INKWELLS

Dips and Drips of Life's Journeys

by

Sage Elders

A COMPILATION from the

SCRIBES AT WORK WRITERS' GUILD

Printed in the Jackson TN, USA

INKWELLS: Dips and Drips of Life's Journeys

Sage Elders is the pen name for the writers of the Scribes at Work (S.A.W.) Writers' Guild. The S.A.W. members who wrote this compilation of stories: T. Callahan, L. Collins, C. Dye, T. Lee, P. Morris, A. Took, D. Vick, and D. Ware.

SAW.SageElders@yahoo.com.

Unless otherwise noted, all Scripture quotations are from the King James Version (KJV) which is a public domain in the United States.

Book Cover Front: SelfPubBookCovers.com/Sierrame
Book Cover Spine/Back: Donna J. Ware

ISBN:979-8-218-32022-5
Library of Congress Control Number: 2023922103

Printed in Jackson, TN, USA • Ingram Spark

Elders, Sage

INKWELLS: Dips and Drips of Life's Journeys—First Edition

Spirituality • Inspiration • Personal Growth

To:

____

From:

____

____

Author Signature

Dedication

We dedicate this work back to our Heavenly Father for His glory, and to you dear reader, for your encouragement, guidance, inspiration, and spiritual growth.

Acknowledgements

Most importantly, Hallelujah, praise and glory to God the Father, Jesus our Savior, and the Holy Spirit's indwelling guidance and counsel, Who has comforted us with healing, strength, and power through this entire endeavor.

With heartfelt love and humility, we pay homage to two of our dear S.A.W. members, Dr. Geraldine Callahan and Adele Vick. Both have done what we all aim to do—they transitioned over into Glory. They have done as the Apostle Paul said, "I have fought the good fight, I have finished the race, I have kept the faith." (2 Timothy 4:7, NIV). We shall miss them forever. Their contributions to our guild, our lives, and the world are priceless.

Thank you to our readers for reading our stories. We pray forever blessings for each of you.

To S.A.W., "Trust in the Lord with all thine heart; and lean not unto thine own understanding. In all thy ways acknowledge him, and he shall direct thy paths." (Proverbs 3:5-6 KJV)

Introduction

Meet the Sage Elders. Actually, "Sage Elders" is our pen name; Scribes at Work (S.A.W.), is our writers' guild name; and *Valley Trudgers, Mountain Climbers, Water Walkers* are our God-ordained, destiny driven Christian faith-in-action names.

At the core of our mission lies the need to write for God's glory, and for our readers' edification, guidance, encouragement, and delight. The accounts in this work share the complexities of our individual life journeys. We reveal that in the eye of every storm, God was with us. As followers of Jesus Christ, we are called and chosen, elected, and selected, anointed, and appointed to share with you what God can do, has done, and will do - not only for us, but for every living soul that loves Jesus Christ as their Lord and Savior.

We have learned through the years the lessons Paula Abdul spoke of when she said, " If you walk in gratitude miracles can happen." We have learned Whitney Houston's lesson: " My mother taught me beauty really lives in places like a smile." And, we have learned, Susan Kelechi Watson's mantra, "You can't go wrong if you choose joy." If you read this work, you can be blessed by so many other life lessons that time and trials have taught us.

We are united not to write for personal accolades, but for God's glory, and for your call to reckon, reason, believe, trust, and obey, for your deliverance, freedom, and spiritual growth. As Sage Elders, our writers' guild is based on the following foundational Scripture: "This is what we speak, not in words taught us by human wisdom but in words taught by the Spirit, explaining spiritual realities with Spirit-taught words." 1 Corinthians 2:13 (NIV).

In these poems, Word unscrambling, brain games, and long and short narratives, truths are told while God's conclusion of each story leads to His pre-destined ends.

It is my privilege to introduce to you the Sage Elders whose work stems from the humble beginnings of the Scribes at Work. My heart is warmed because the group God asked me to establish in 2013 continues to grow, follow God's voice, and prosper. Dear readers, blessings to each of you and yours.

With Christian love,

Donna J. Ware
Founding Leader, Scribes at Work (S.A.W.)
Sage Elder
Texas Indie Author of ten books

Table of Contents

ACKNOWLEDGMENTS

INTRODUCTION

POETRY 13

It's All About Our Journey 14

Deliverance Came Down 15

Flight From Yourself Is Not An Option 19

A Mother's Love 20

God, You Are The Diamond Of My Life 21

I Am In The Right Hands 22

Adam Where Are You? 23

I Believe 26

I Give God The Credit 27

My Seasons Changed 28

Should Have Died 29

We Are Children Of God 30

This Too, Soon Shall Pass 31

Air and Earth 32

I Woke Up This Morning 34

Growth Is 35

SHORT STORIES - FICTION 37

You Will Know Them By Their Fruit 38

In The Night 40

Did You Consult God? 43

Why Me? 46

GAMES AND BRAIN TEASERS 49

1 Crossword Puzzle 50

2 Jumble Words 52

3 Word Search 53

4 Crypto Quotes 54

5 Solutions 55

Copyright Information for Games 60

REFLECTIONS   61

We Are Capable Of Change   62

Wisdom Keys   66

What I Know At 75   69

LONG STORY - FICTION   75

When The Vow Breaks   76

SHORT STORIES NON-FICTION   83

Be Careful With Your Words   84

A Strong Black Woman Final Weeks Tribute   87

A Student Stood Up To Adversity   89

Final Weeks Tribute with Poem - "Wanna Ride?"   91

I Am Proud Of Myself   94

Have You Heard About Rahab?   96

No Time To Waste   99

We Take It For Granted   101

Prayer For Healing   104

My Mom Is Still In The House   108

Sipping Sufficient Grace   109

Secret   112

Why?   114

Self-Worth   116

A Disciplined Prayer Life   118

My Family Reunion   122

Soul Testing   125

Women In Positions Once Held By Men   127

<u>LONG STORIES NON-FICTION</u>   129

Broken Glass   130

Courageous Women of African-American Descent   141

Let Me Tell You About The Blue Room   148

Prayer For Change   152

Overcoming Challenges   156

Holy Living   162

Reasons To Keep On Living   167

Learn To Pray With Power   172

Where Are The Greatest Minds?   177

Is It God's Favor Or Not?   181

MAMA SAID - Roundtable Quotes   185

CONCLUSION   195

AUTHOR BIOGRAPHIES   199

OTHER BOOKS BY THE AUTHORS   205

BOOK RELEASES IN 2024   207

POETRY

Our life journeys are told in poetry.

My story can only be told by me, and nobody has to agree with it. – Lauren Ridloff

It's All About Our Journey
By Patricia Ann Callahan Morris

It's all about our journey,
our lives and work,
while we daily face injustices.

We will not stand in silence, though.
We will not accept that nothing can be changed.
We know our journey is difficult,
as our past has historically shown.
Yet, we continue to work each day for the
betterment of future generations.

We endured all. Even so, "We Rise" and continue to
move forward despite the disparities against us.
We will bear no arms against anyone.
Instead, we keep on by praying for God's guidance.

In the past, I placed my shoes under the *bed,*
to ensure I said my daily prayers before I laid down.
Now, I place my shoes under my *chair,*
and I lean forward to pray and
to thank God before I lay down.

This is my journey, and maybe yours, as it is today.

Deliverance Came Down

By Tjuana Ladawn Callahan

Suddenly . . . deliverance came down.

He was there all the time,

standing steadfast and ready . . .

waiting for the call.

Ain't God Good!

You've got my attention.

There was peaceful silence.

Then I heard the crash of strongholds

breaking beneath the deliverance call.

Like broken glass hitting the floor

Like shattered glass

Breaking through lies

Breaking through shame

Breaking through heart aches

Breaking through chains

It's time to write.

Ain't God Good!

Supernaturally

Miraculously

Suddenly . . .

No . . . He was there all the time

waiting for the exact moment.

And now is the time

for deliverance.

Break the shackles of defeat.

Now is the time

for salvation.

GOD IS with us

in the flesh.

He was there all the time.

But He needed to get our attention.

Suddenly . . . Jesus came.

And the angel appeared

to the shepherds who were

waiting for deliverance.

And the star appeared

to the wise men seeking

The King of Salvation.

But He was there all the time,

waiting for the precise moment

The time had come;

the time IS now

for deliverance and salvation.

Ain't God Good!

GOD IS with us in the flesh.

He was there all the time!

But some could not see Him!

At last, it was clear, He said,

"I am the Way - The Truth

And the Life!"

Suddenly, an angel appeared.

He was always there

watching and waiting

for the appointed time.

And she . . . was chosen

to give birth to the Son of God.

GOD IS with us!

Salvation is ready!

Receive Him today!

She said, yes, I am willing.

But I don't understand how.

Listen . . . the Holy Spirit will come

in supernatural, miraculous power!

He was always there

waiting and watching

for the anointed time.

Let deliverance come! She said,

I receive it today!

Be it unto me just as you say!

I <u>am</u> your servant,

Be it unto me!

There is nothing impossible with God!

Then, Mary received, and she conceived.

Mary received salvation.

She carried the babe within her womb

until the term was due.

Then miraculously she gave birth

and deliverance came down from

heaven to earth.

Hallelujah, AMEN

Flight From Yourself
Is Not An Option

By Patricia Ann Callahan-Morris

Averting one's eyes from the unpalatable,
it is not possible to run away.
You will be present when you arrive.

Face up to your reflection.
You can't run; it will persist.
You can't run; face yourself when you get there.

Enjoy each day you awaken.
Start your day with a purpose.
It is a new day.
Make the best of it for yourself and no one else.
Smile, even when it is difficult to smile.

You can't escape yourself.
You can't run away from yourself because you are still
there when you get there.
You are still yourself when you get there.

A Mother's Love

By Denise Vick

Never ending love.
Regardless of what you do or say,
through pain and sorrow,
Mother still loves you.

A mother's love
can bear the weight
of thousands of pounds' worth of
Letdowns, heartbreaks and even "Hate You's."

No matter how toxic you become.
Regardless of the many acidic burns.
A true mother continues to love.
You are her gift from God.

A mother's love is second only
to Jesus' love for us.
There should be no hatred,
even when you have to "let go and let God."

A mother's love
is always prayerful,
constantly hopeful,
never-ending.

A mother's love,
is fueled by faith,
moved by the Holy Ghost,
sustained by Jesus Christ.

God, You Are The Diamond
In My Life

By Patricia Ann Callahan Morris

God, You are the diamond in my life.
You are Who You are, no matter where I am.
I may try to bear physical pain with every drop of my tears.
Gratefully, You are there to relieve my pain.

You see me when my life is going great.
You see me when life is complicated.
You see me every moment of the day and night.
I know You are Who You are.

You are there during the dark times in my life.
You carry me into the light.
God, You are the diamond in my life.

I praise You forever,
no matter where I am.
God, You are the diamond in my life.
You are the Alpha and the Omega.
God, You are the diamond in my life.

I Am In The Right Hands

By Patricia Ann Callahan Morris

When others thought I would fail without them,
I was in the right hands.

When faced with raising two boys as a single parent,
I was in the right hands.

Worries about meeting obligations,
 I am in the right hands.

Praying in the night God's presence is there,
I am in the right hands.

My life's journey takes on a new meaning:
I am in the right hands.

Adam, Where Are You?

By Tjuana Ladawn Callahan

Adam, why are you hiding,
wandering from place to place?
Why did you move from the garden,
away from God's grace?
Adam, "Where are you?"
Are you hiding in guilt and shame?
Have you missed the mark of the promise?
Have you forgotten your name?
Adam, I have a plan for you.
Be still and know Who, I AM.
I created you with purpose,
to rule over this land.
But you turned it over
into Satan's hand.

Cain, why are you roaming,
drifting like the wind?
Where's the place you call home?
Where is your next of kin?
Cain, "Where is your brother?"
I know what you have done.
Jealousy was the culprit.
Rage led you on.
Murder took over,
now, your brother is gone.
I created you with power;

to plant and to build.
But you used that strength
to tear down and kill.

Hagar, where do you think you're going?
Why are you running away?
You are indispensable,
therefore, you must stay.
I know it's been hard.
I see what's going on.
You've been used and abused
but just hold on.
I created you with life
to birth us a nation.
To face adversity
with dignity and patience.

Wandering.
Drifting.
Running Away . . .
It was never meant to
be this way.

Don't be a drifter,
blowing in the wind.
Lay your foundation.
Build up your walls.
Rooted and grounded,
resilient and strong.

With a call to answer

and a purpose to fulfill,
put down your anchor
and be still.
Facing guilt and shame,
jealousy and rage,
use and abuse,
heartache and pain.

Come now
let us reason together,
though your sins
are blood red.
I will make them
white as snow.

Please don't keep running.
What was meant to kill you
will only make you stronger.
I have a plan for you
of hope and restoration,
of prosperity and greatness,
to bring you safely home.

I Believe

By Patricia Ann Callahan Morris

When people told me to forget my dream and give up Pat. It's never going to happen. I believed.

I know the doors may be closed at the present,
but whenever they open, I will be prepared for
when that opportunity arises and walks in.

I know God's presence is always with me.
I may not see Him, but do feel His presence,
as I sit quietly to listen for His whisper.

My mind focuses on when Moses went to the
mountain and saw the "Burning Bush."
He returned from the mountain holding
The Ten Commandments, God transcribed
onto the stone tablets.
It was God Who spoke from the "Burning Bush."

I Give God The Credit

By Patricia Ann Callahan Morris

I give God the credit for all He has given me.
I credit God for all His blessings and grace toward me.
I give God the credit and shout, "I love You, God!"

He comforts me when I am feeling sad.
He brings joy, calmness, and inner peace.
He picks me up when I fall.
He reminds me He is here holding my hand.

I give God the credit every day.
He wakes me up to face another day.
He hears my prayers in the wee hours of the night.
I give God the credit.

I share and express my blessings through songs and prayers
while praising Him.
I give Him all the Glory.
I give God the credit.

My Seasons Changed

By Patricia Ann Callahan Morris

We can't change our past, but we can change our future. Our lives mimic the four seasons: fall, winter, spring, and summer, each bringing significant changes.

I have not been perfect, but I have been faithful. I know that if I haven't, I will reap what I sow.

My season changed. When I felt the verge of falling; bewildered by my decision. I reached out to God for guidance to help me not to backslide.

My season changed. When the cold came upon me. I knew I planted my seeds deep enough that my blessings were stored and protected by God's favor and would be there in the spring.

My season changed. It brought forth more of nature's beauty to surround me with the warmth of His breath blowing gentled puffs.

So, I appreciate all the season changes God has revealed to me. It helps me strive to be a better person, while serving others whenever possible.

My seasons changed.

Should Have Died

By Denise Vick

I should have died.
You will hear people say,
No, not true.

For if you should have died,
you can rest assured
that you would have died.
I almost died,
is another false statement.
And here again, not true.

There is no almost
when referring to life or death.
You are either dead or alive.

That was a close one.
Phew, I thought I was gone.
Really? Where is your faith?

Have you got a firm grip-
tight hold on His hand?
Who's hands are you holding?

My God, My God
has told me I am His,
so don't believe them.

You said I should have died.
God said, "No."
So I said, "No."

We Are Children Of God

By Patricia Ann Callahan Morris

We are children of God.
He keeps all His promises.
When we feel down and out.
He is coming, no doubt.
There is nothing he cannot resolve.

If you bring it to God leave it in His Hands.
He fixes everything completely.
He has proven all he says in the Scriptures.
"I Am," yes, "I Am."
So bring to and leave your troubles with Him.

Because we are the children of God.
We can count on Him,
for all life's trials and tribulations.

This Too Soon Shall Pass
By Patricia Ann Callahan Morris

When I feel that pain will never end.
This too soon shall pass.

The goals I have set forth are unattainable.
This too soon shall pass.

When I have doubts about my decision.
This too soon shall pass.

When I feel anxious.
This too soon shall pass.

When I don't know the answer.
This too soon shall pass.

When I am overwhelmed by the passing of someone I love.
This too soon shall pass.

When time passes too fast to do all I like in a day.
This too soon shall pass.

Time passing can be my best ally by prioritizing instead.
This too soon shall pass.[1]

---

[1] This saying is believed to be based on a Persian adage passed down throughout time made famous in 1852 with Edward Fitzgerald's "Solomon's Seal." In it, King Solomon aims to create a sentence that will always be true-whether times are good or bad. In it, he responds" This too, soon will pass away."

Air and Earth

By Patricia Ann Callahan Morris

We struggle with the rapid changes in air and earth.
These changes are occurring in our flat lands, mountains,
rivers, and lakes.

They have uprooted "Mother Nature" and replaced it with
concrete with highways, more than you can imagine.
The skyscrapers and parking decks replaced our family's
homes.

Air and Earth

What other changes will occur before our very eyes
between our philosophy of humankind change in the air
and earth?
Our heads spin in the wonder of what can happen next
between air and the earth.

The food changes make it difficult for a single parent to
feed and keep a roof over their children's heads.
The gas prices change every week cause families to cancel
family activities once enjoyed on weekends.

Our justice system is like a whirlwind of easy accessibility
of assault weapons taking the lives of our innocent

children, whose only mindset is to learn and never return to that school bus and home.

These are the circumstances we face every day occurring in the air and earth.
We should be ashamed of all our gifts of God, because we enjoy living in peace within the air and earth.

I Woke Up This Morning
By Patricia Ann Callahan Morris

*It is when we take just waking up as a given but not as a blessing;
someone else planned for today, but they did not wake up.*

I woke up this morning with a smile on my face.
Sat on the side of my bed and recited my prayers for today.
Then took a shower and got dressed to be on my way.
I made some breakfast which started my day.

I kept a smile on my face all day.
Sat down at my desk, thinking about what to write about
today.
I kept that smile on my face all day.

I can't stop thinking about God for another day.
He allowed me to wake up for another day with a smile on
my face.

Growth Is . . .

By Tjuana Ladawn Callahan

Growth is change.
It's transformation.
It's a never-ending progress.
Constant moving,
swift or small.

Like babies we adore . . .
First steps become baby steps.
Baby steps grow into big steps.
Before we know it, he's
running all over the place.

Just like that child . . .
growth is falling down
and getting back up
again and again,
realizing errors, mistakes, and failures.
Growth is forgiving the past and
being humbled enough to change.

Growth is patience.
A lifelong journey of time;
death is the end of growth.
A listener and a learner
is always growing.

Growth is obedience to wisdom
following through to completion.

Like weight lifting develops muscle,
growth is heavy and growing pain is real.

Body weight leads to dumb bells.
Dumb bells lead to bar bells.
Challenges become greater.
Weight becomes heavier.
Endurance and repetition
produce strength.

Growth is persistent.
Ability leads to responsibility.
Responsibility becomes reliability.
And reliability produces maturity.
It's the never-ending process called life.
Growth is risking faith for the future
with hope for change.

SHORT STORIES

FICTION

Life journeys told in fiction short stories.

According to Mark Twain, "Truth is stranger than fiction, but it is because Fiction is obliged to stick to possibilities; Truth isn't."[2]

---

[2] www.goodreads.com/quotes/4650-truth-is-stranger-than-fiction. Accessed November 14, 2023.

You Will Know Them
By Their Fruit
By Lillian Collins

Abby tries to do God's will by volunteering to help underprivileged students. The students love Abby because they feel she understands them. Abby came from a disadvantaged home herself. Her mother smoked crack cocaine, and her dad was in prison. Abby loved her parents, but decided that her life would be very different. Abby's grandmother always told her she was beautiful inside and outside. Her grandmother told her to set her sights on greatness, courage, and love.

Abby constantly helps her students by encouraging them to do their best every day. She shows them what love and caring are about. They are a team. Even if the school sometimes ignored their needs, Abby teaches them the best way she can.

Some of her friends rarely understood why she remained at the sub-standard school. She could make so much more money and not have to work as hard at a school where children had all the tools for success. Her friends would turn their noses up at her and not invite her to affluent social events.

Out of all Abby's students, one student struggled to get by with her lessons. Abby worked with that student every day after class. She poured all her strength into that student. Her name was Krystal. Abby would explain to her that her name was precious and beautiful. She explained that there was nothing she could not accomplish. She had to work hard, pray to GOD, and love herself and others.

Today Krystal is the principal at the high school where she graduated. She often acknowledges Ms. Abby. She poured her love and encouragement into Krystal to be great, work hard, and pray to GOD. Krystal is just one of Abby's students who went far in life for success.

You will know them by their fruit.

In The Night

By Lillian Collins

It was dark, cold, and raining. Lois walked faster and faster to get away. Was there someone following her? It was just in her mind, of course. She always imagined the dumbest things. But then again, what was that noise behind her? Lois could not and would not look back behind her. What if someone was following her? What did they want? Surely, she did not look prosperous.

Actually, her shoes were runover, her coat was tattered, and her umbrella barely kept the rain off of her. Keep walking, she told herself. Keep walking faster and faster. Where was she going anyway in the wee hours of the night? Why was Lois out there in the dark, rainy, frosty night?

Lois got an urgent call from a friend. *"Lois, please help me. I need you right away. I cannot tell you over the phone. You must come, and you will not regret coming."* Her friend would never ask her to come out on a dark rainy night unless it was extremely important. What would be so crucial that Lois risk going out in the cold at night? Someone was following Lois. She was sure of it, but her friend needed her right away.

It must have been a good thing because why would Rose say, *"it was extremely important?"* Lois started running now, faster and faster. She was almost there. Just a little further. She had to make it to her friend's house because it was crucial, and she would not regret it. Whatever was following Lois, it kept right behind her. She could not look back into the dark, cold night. It was too frightening to imagine. The rain blinded her eyes, but she had to make it.

Finally, she made it to Rose's house. She still did not look back into the dark and rain. Why didn't Rose have her lights on? Where was Rose? Lois knocked as hard and loudly as she could because whoever was following her came closer and closer. Lois's heart was pounding as she hit harder and harder.

Just as Rose opened the door, the dog ran into the house, shaking and wet, looking up at Lois while wagging his tail and showing love on its face. Lois went to the door to look back and saw nothing. She kneeled and kissed her dog.

"Okay, what was so important, Rose, that you got me out in the dark, cold wee hours of the night?" Rose looked at Lois with a big smile, showing the gap in her teeth, and spoke. *"Look Lois at*

my finger. Alvin and I are engaged, and we want you to be my maid of honor."

I wanted you to be the first to know because you are my best friend." *Lois was stunned. Rose and Alvin had been dating for a long time. Lois used to ask Rose, "When are you guys going to tie the knot? You know your mom would not approve of your living together." Rose said, "I know, and I wish she could have been here. We set a date for May 15th, Lois. That was the day she passed away." Lois said, "I know. She will be smiling from heaven. I do not regret running here in the dark, cold wee hours of the night."*

Did You Consult God?
By *Lillian Collins*

It was a beautiful, sunny day, without a cloud in the sky. Lisa King was reflecting on the day she became the most powerful woman in her company. She had no regrets and had earned the applause and admiration of her staff. Lisa had just won the highest award that a woman had ever won at BCD Enterprises. She *"took no prisoners"* because she did what she had to do to win. Yes, she had to step on a few toes to get to the top, but she would not apologize for what she had done. That was business.

Everyone knows it is difficult to achieve greatness. The *"Woman of the Year Award"* was given to Lisa King. She was getting a gold plaque and a $50,000 monetary award.

Lisa King was the oldest child in her family. She was confident, and beautiful, and had graduated at the top of her class. Lisa had made a five-year plan to own her own marketing firm at thirty years old. She was on track to do what no other person had done in her family, which was to be worth over one million dollars. Lisa worked very hard with long hours at the office, and she pushed her staff to work just as hard.

This beautiful sunny day was her moment, and she was so proud of herself for what she had achieved. It did not matter that she did not pray or think about her struggling family. This award was what she had planned and worked hard for it. What did it matter that her family had a crisis? Lisa ignored the warning signs. It was about her, and her alone.

The family called to say that Fannie King, her mother, had a stroke. How could this happen the day after Lisa won her award? She was on top of the world now. No, no, nothing was going to spoil her achievement. She had planned a trip to go to the islands to relax and wallow in her achievements. How dare her mother have a stroke and ruin this time in her life? This was not fair.

Who said she couldn't have peace and happiness, plus that "*rose garden*?" She had reached her goal of success with the award she had just won. Her motto was "When a lemon comes your way, you make lemonade". Lisa told her family to take care of their mother, and that she would return in a week. Again, she had worked too hard for this, and nothing was going to stop her.

Lisa went on her trip and had a wonderful time. She ate exotic foods, met some wonderful people, and spent a lot of money doing *"her thing."* Lisa planned her next big assignment on her return flight. She was confident that everything would be all right at home. Unfortunately, the plane was hijacked. Mayhem broke out on the plane, and Lisa thought about her mother and family back home. Too bad for Lisa because it was too late to notify her family that she was traveling.

All the awards she had won and all her accolades from BCD did not matter. All Lisa's money could not save her now. It was the *"end of the road"* for Lisa King. Sadly, she did not know how to pray. It was still a bright, sunny day, with not a cloud in the sky. Lisa King died that day. Her plane never made it home. It crashed into the ocean with all her riches.

Why Me?

By Lillian Collins

I met a woman today, sitting on a turned-over grocery cart while lying under a large leafy tree at a Walmart grocery store. I do not know why my heart went out to this woman on this particular day. I noticed her before lying under this same tree at Walmart, and even if I did not want to gaze at her, my eyes would go there like forbidden fruit.

She is right there on the ground for all to see, and even if I did not want to look at her, I could not miss her. Her belongings were next to her in another cart consisting of food, clothing, and various things customers had donated to her. Her whole life's belongings were in that cart.

She was a large woman with artificial dreadlocks that appeared frayed, dirty, and uncombed. I did not know her pitiful story and, furthermore, did not care because I just wanted to get my groceries and leave. I was surprised that she was lying on the ground under the tree again. Was she ill? Most of the time, beggars would stand up with a sign reading "Help Me". As I drove by her, I wanted to completely forget this uncomfortable scene.

As the Holy Spirit often did, it convicted deep me down in my stomach, like a nagging toothache. So, I circled around to check on her. Coincidently, it was the week before Easter Sunday, and I just had religious tracks in my car. Just then, it began to rain. At that moment, I picked up the tracks along with my umbrella and proceeded towards this woman. I was hesitant to approach her, but I did.

I stood over her with my umbrella raised to shield myself, as well as her from the rain. She looked up at me with sad eyes, swollen lips, and missing front teeth. I tried not to stare in shock and gave her the tracks and some money. I did not intend to start a conversation, but she started talking to me. She thanked me and confessed that she knew about GOD. She said that she had trusted some people offering her a place to stay and gave them all her money. They beat her and left her body broken, hurt, and with no money.

The hotel across the street needed seventy dollars ($70.00) a day for a bed and toilet for her to stay there. She was tired and sick and just felt like life was so hard sometimes. I listened intently to her story as I stood under the large, sprawling tree. It was at that moment that I realized that for the grace of GOD, it could be me. Then, the question, why me, and the answer came back to me, why not you? My mouth echoed the words to her, "GOD bless you, and I walked away from her with tears in my eyes filled with guilt.

GAMES & BRAIN TEASERS

Our journeys worked out in games using "life words".

CROSSWORD PUZZLE
Personality Traits

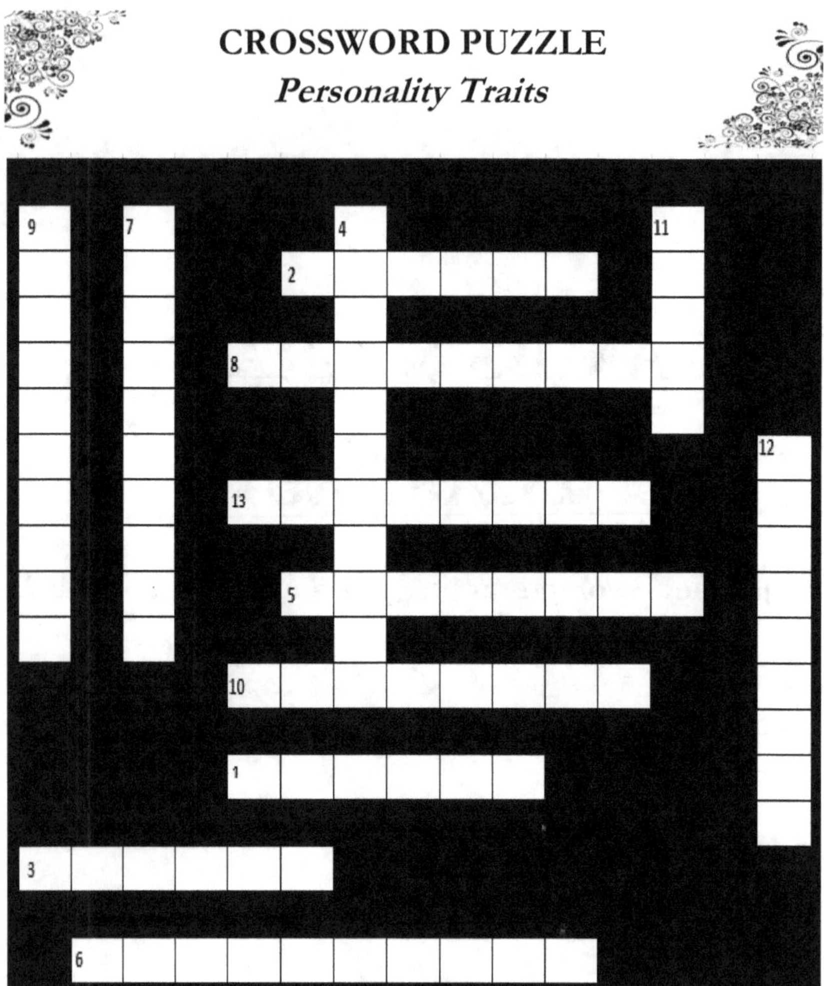

See clues on the next page.

Across

1 Rare and extraordinary
2 Truthful and ethical of matters
3 Civilized, cordial and courteous
5 Sober minded and level headed
6 Confident not easily influenced by others
8 Overcome obstacles and bounce back from
  difficulties
10 Manners that are pleasing
13 Imaginative and original

Down

4 Show kindness to others
7 Fixed, unmoved & persistent
9 Confident about the future
11 Bound to keep peace
12 Practical & sensible to
  achieve goals

JUMBLE WORDS
Family Jumble Words

1. RPSAETN _______________________

2. ULRHTAEG _______________________

3. LATVEIERS _______________________

4. ORFSTE RASPNET _______________________

5. RTESA _______________________

6. EVDEOTD _______________________

7. ISOEECHV _______________________

8. MLTIANSNETE _______________________

9. DRSVEEER _______________________

10. THGERGAIN _______________________

11. CETSOANSR _______________________

12. FNTEAOTIFCEA _______________________

13. UIONRNE _______________________

14. RCDNEHIL _______________________

15. ADSAFTTES _______________________

16. YYASDTN _______________________

WORD SEARCH PUZZLE

T	P	U	N	C	H	S	P	I	H	C
R	E	W	V	C	A	N	D	Y	A	B
E	S	I	N	G	I	N	G	H	M	N
A	F	N	U	G	J	V	F	T	B	I
T	A	Y	O	L	K	S	O	S	U	C
S	M	O	H	O	U	S	E	T	R	E
D	I	U	F	W	L	A	D	F	G	C
E	L	S	R	C	Y	L	G	I	E	R
C	Y	V	I	M	V	K	A	G	R	E
O	Y	K	E	A	G	K	Z	B	S	A
R	O	G	N	S	E	K	A	C	N	M
A	K	V	D	L	H	X	N	W	P	E
T	B	P	S	S	G	O	D	T	O	H
I	T	U	N	A	S	A	L	A	D	H
O	H	Q	S	E	L	D	N	A	C	R
N	P	G	M	G	A	M	E	S	J	N
S	D	V	L	C	I	S	U	M	P	G

BALLOONS	FRIENDS	HOT DOGS
CAKE	FAMILY	CHIPS
CANDY	HAMBURGER	TUNA SALAD
ICE CREAM	CANDLES	MUSIC
GAMES	HOUSE	GIFTS
DECORATIONS	PUNCH	SINGING
	TREATS	

Cryptograms Quotes

A	B	C	D	E	F	G	H	I	J	K	L	M	N	O	P	Q	R	S	T	U	V	W	X	Y	Z
P	R	Y	B	W	M	U	S	O	G	E	I	Q	D	H	K	L	A	Z	V	X	C	F	N	J	T

USE LETTERS WITH THE BOLD FACE ON FIRST ROW OF THE GRID TO DECODE LETTER IN THE TEXT

1. "Lw cig zrqp zi r frx lx r qrxjgrjk ok gxnkbhzrxnh, zorz jikh zi olh okrn. Lw cig zrqp zi olf lx olh qrxjgrjk, zorz jikh zi olh okrbz."
Nelson Mandela

"If you talk…" __________________________
____
____
____

2. "Frx lh gqzlfrzkqc hgakblib zi rxc fkvorxlvrq nktlvk."
James T. Kirk

____
____
____
____

3. "Cig nix'z zkqq nkqldkbrzk qlkh, dgz hifkzlfkh cig ortk zi dk ktrhltk."
Margaret Thatcher

____
____
____
____

SOLUTIONS

SOLUTIONS
Crossword

SOLUTIONS
Jumbles Words

1. PARENTS
2. LAUGHTER
3. RELATIVES
4. FOSTER PARENTS
5. TEARS
6. DEVOTED
7. COHESIVE
8. SENTIMENTAL
9. RESERVED
10. GATHERING
11. ANCESTORS
12. AFFECTIONATE
13. RE-UNION
14. CHILDREN
15. STEADFAST
16. DYNASTY

SOLUTIONS
Word Search

T	P	U	N	C	H	S	P	I	H	C
R				C	A	N	D	Y	A	
E	S	I	N	G	I	N	G		M	
A	F	N							B	I
T	A		O					S	U	C
S	M		H	O	U	S	E	T	R	E
D	I		F		L			F	G	C
E	L		R			L		I	E	R
C	Y		I				A	G	R	E
O			E		K		B	S	A	
R			N		E	K	A	C		M
A			D							
T			S	S	G	O	D	T	O	H
I	T	U	N	A	S	A	L	A	D	
O			S	E	L	D	N	A	C	
N				G	A	M	E	S		
S				C	I	S	U	M		

BALLOONS   FRIENDS   HOT DOGS
CAKE   FAMILY   CHIPS
CANDY   HAMBURGER   TUNA SALAD
ICE CREAM   CANDLES   MUSIC
GAMES   HOUSE   GIFTS
DECORATIONS   PUNCH   SINGING
   TREATS

SOLUTIONS

Cryptograms Quotes

1. "If you talk to a man in a language
   he understands, that goes to his head. If
   you talk to him in his language, that goes
   to his heart."
   Nelson Mandela

2. "Man is ultimately superior to any
   mechanical device."
   James T. Kirk

3. "You don't tell deliberate lies, but
   sometimes you have to be evasive."
   Margaret Thatcher

For each of the included games:

REFLECTIONS

Thoughtful moments

about our life journeys.

"Finish each day and be done with it. You have done what
you could. Some blunders and absurdities no doubt crept
in; forget them as soon as you can. Tomorrow is a new day.
You shall begin it serenely and with too high a spirit to be
encumbered with your old nonsense."[3]
— Ralph Waldo Emerson

---

[3] www.goodreads.com/quotes/life. Accessed November 7, 2023.

We Are Capable Of Change

By Patricia Ann Callahan Morris

We can change the ways we learn and can-do things better if we are open to becoming more knowledgeable and sharing these simple guidelines: I will not preach, but teach by sharing the ways if you accompany me on this learning journey.

It is pleasurable to gain knowledge of new information. Facts, concepts, and skills gained through various resources, such as textbooks, online seminars, discussions with friends, and other resources, keep life interesting.

Stimulating your brain and heart awakens your senses to real-life situations.

Oh! Using critical thinking to review, consider, and develop solutions can help you create a better life for yourself.

Oh! The emotions swirl within you like a waterfall, both visible and invisible to the human eye, and it feels like rivers that will never end.

Yes. You have incorporated newfound knowledge, providing the impetus to make wiser decisions in your life than you ever have before.

Constant practice and honing your skills will help you become the master of your dreams, so don't dwell on the past, focus on the future.

Those around you have observed the changes you have made and are curious to know what has enhanced your life.

As each day passed, you felt more motivated to step out and embrace the unknown with greater faith, thankfulness, and obedience than ever before.

Self-reflection and continued practice are vital for learning and development during life's journey.

He Needs No Introduction
By Patricia Ann Callahan Morris

- He is already well-known and needs no introduction. (See Luke 2:9-11)

- He had two incredible parents, Joseph and Mary. (See Luke 2:4-5)

- He was born in a barn in Bethlehem. (Luke 2:4-7)

- Three wise men to see Him. (See Matthew 2:11)

- At age twelve, He went into the temple. He sat among the teachers. (See Luke 2:46)

- He fed four - thousand with seven loaves of bread and fish. (See Matthew 15:36-37)

- He walked the waters. (See Matthew 14:22-34; Mark 6:45-53; and John 6:15-21)

- He meditated for forty days and triumphed. (See Matthew 4:1-11)

- He is the light of the world. (See John 8:12)

- He turns water into wine. (See John 2:6-9)

- God shall supply all our needs according to His riches in glory by Christ Jesus. (See Philippians 4:19)

- At Calvary, he died on the cross for our sins. (See Corinthians 15: 3-5)
- He was buried, and on the third, he rose again. (See John 2:19-20)
- He is the Son of God, JESUS! (See Matthew 16:16)
- He is the Alpha and the Omega (See Revelation 1:8)
- Jesus is ALIVE! (See Revelation 1:7)
- God is coming back. (See Acts 1:10-11)[4]

So, I wait, kneel, and give Him praise for His Love. Hallelujah!

---

[4] All Scriptures were excerpted from the Holy Bible, New International Version.

Wisdom Keys
By Annette Tooks

- Learn to be a thermostat, not a thermometer.

- You control and set the temperature.

- You are the total of the choices you make.

- You can control the choices you make, but not the circumstances.

- Use faith in every area of your life. Building faith is like building muscle for strength.

- Then and now. Stop looking in the rearview mirror to compare your progress. Keep looking forward.

- Learn to face your fears. Fear is often the test of faith. When we walk in faith, we walk through the valley of fear.

- The Holy Spirt uses the word of God as an instrument of change in your life.

- Your obedience to the word of God will determine your success with faith. (See Psalms 1:19) He who is willing and obedient shall eat the fat of the land.

- IGNORANCE is DEADLY. Know that God is a God of wisdom and knowledge. (See Hosea 4:6) A lack of knowledge destroyed not the lies, demons, or sexual perversions. IGNORANCE: (See James 1:5) "If any man lacks wisdom, let him ask of God that giveth to all men liberally without finding fault. I will give you what you ask for. When you ask, you must BELIEVE and not doubt!"

- Your words can become a self-fulfilled prophecy. WATCH what you say.

- Trust GOD. Know that when GOD says NO, he's protecting you. TRUST GOD.

- WAIT ON GOD. Be still to hear and know HE is working. He's got this! (See Psalms 27:14) "Wait on GOD be of good courage, and he shall strengthen your heart, WAIT I SAY on the LORD."

- Never say I'm on a fixed income. Our GOD is not a Father of lack. The last time I checked HE "owns all the cattle on a thousand hills." (See Psalm 50:10) Our words become a self-fulfilled prophecy. What do you BELIEVE?

- Successful people do daily what unsuccessful people do occasionally.

- The proof of love is the willingness to forgive, correct wrongs, and move forward.

- What you keep speaking you will eventually believe.

- Your reaction to the word of GOD determines your and your family's success.

- Seize the moment of opportunity. Trust GOD to provide what's needed for the task ahead. Please take note, this moment may never happen again.

- Renew your mind. Do a quarterly checkup. Ask these three questions: Where was I THEN? Where am I NOW? Where am I going NEXT? Now grab your pen and paper and wait on the HOLY SPIRIT to download his directive for HE KNOWS ALL THINGS. JUST ASK.

At 75, I Know…

By Donna J. Ware

- Foremost, I cry rivers, oceans, and seas full of tears of gratefulness for living to see seventy-five years.

- I am simply in awe of God's love for sparing me to see seventy-five years.

- When I say it, I think to myself, hmmm… 75 years, 3/4th century, 7 ½ decades, 3,900 weeks, 27,450 days, 658,800 hours, and 39,528,000 seconds. I am blessed.

- For sixty-seven years, from age eight, I am blessed to have accepted Jesus Christ into my heart as my Lord and Savior.

- In the words from the song, Mother Sandy Wilson used to sing frequently, "Just another day, the Lord has kept me!"

- I know each day is a precious gift from God. Cancer brought me closer to God than humanly thought to be possible. I could not bargain for a longer life, but claiming three Scriptures that spoke life to me, God brought to me in my hospital bed, radiation from heaven. Going on forty-three years ago, God healed me, and life gained a new level of *preciousness* to and for me. It is a gift to realize, use, and rejoice in every day.

- One thing I know, family is a treasure to love, honor, trust, respect, enjoy, and love some more.

- I know friends-both old and new, are a gift. God allowed our paths to cross for His reasons and purposes, and for our benefit and enjoyment.

- I know I have a pre-ordained purpose. My destiny lies before me. My job is to tread my destiny path, follow my heart and God's guidance.

- I know seventy-five got here too quickly. I need to live another fifty to seventy-five to write all the books God has assigned me to write, and to do all the things I already know to be my destiny steps.

- I know this world has become the most unsafe place possible. Each day, I must put on my full armor of God. Every day, no matter what happens, I must give God gratitude. I must allow Him to fight my battles, for with His power, all my battles are already won.

- The best way to live is to do at least one thing that makes me happy or brings me joy each day. My

Grandma Martha Lee Stills told me this almost every day from the time I was a tiny tot until I got married. After which, she wrote it to me in weekly letters until she passed in 1981.

- I know putting God first gives me the life He intended me to have; one full of challenges, successes and failures, but one where He is in control, and He has His best planned for me.

- I have learned that when God sets up a provision, never challenge it or try to change or upgrade it. Accept it with grace and live entirely therein. He always has the best plan.

- I have learned I get what I pray for; when I pray, without doubt, with complete faith, nothing is impossible with God. In praying, pray for exactly what I want. Pray a complete and detailed plea, except in dire emergencies, when simply calling on "Jesus" is all heaven needs to rescue me.

- I have learned that my life is really not about me, but is a channel through which God can complete His purposes.

- If I start my day with prayer, counting my blessings, my day will be God-ordained, God-protected, God-directed, a grace and favor-filled to the brim kind of day to bring me that hoped for unspeakable joy.

- I know beyond all doubt that "every day with Jesus" as my Lord and Savior "gets sweeter as the days go by."

- I have learned to visualize a place that makes me happy, feast my mind's eye upon it and set up camp. This helps me through the most intense fiery trials.

- Even at 75, medical situations still embarrass me. But embarrassment does not kill us. I've learned to accept it as simply part of real living.

- Each day, I should seek to help someone. Being kind, praying for others, and lending a helping hand are showing God's love in action. God expects us to do these things.

- We each have a purpose. If we do not know what it is, we need to seek God's face until He reveals it to us, or until destiny steps present themselves and the right doors open. This all requires trusting God.

- Please be kind to our loved ones by drafting our last will and testament, medical directive, and any other end-of-life documents. Notarize these and store them in a safe deposit box, or with a law firm, fire-proof box, or a safe place. Confirm your Durable Power of Attorney (person of your choice) is aware of said location.

- If I listen to God, He will guide me through any situation or problem. He will show me the right way, open the right door, make the provisions available to me, close the wrong door, and guide me all the way through his perfect answer.

- I've learned that experiences can be the best gifts.

- Nearing seventy-six, I know beyond all doubt that nothing really counts or matters but what we do for God and His glory, in obedience to His will, ways, and timing.

- I know the best blessing a parent can receive is for their offspring to know Jesus as their Lord and Savior, and that they are trying each day to live for God's glory.

- Please be kind to our loved ones by drafting our last will and testament, medical directive, and any other end-of-life documents. Get them notarized and store them in a safe deposit box, or with a law firm, fireproof box, or a safe place. Confirm your Durable Power of Attorney (DPOA) as a person of your choosing. Make sure they know the location of your "important papers."

- One thing I know beyond all doubt, this world as we know it will pass away. Jesus will come again in the sky to collect all us saints–those dead and those alive. God will give us new spiritual bodies in a twinkling of an eye. We will go to heaven to collect those rewards. We will stand before the *Judgment Seat of Christ*, where we receive our rewards. God, Jesus, and the Holy Spirit will *not* bring our old failings to mind. God has thrown them into the sea of forgetfulness. Hallelujah, thank You Jesus.

- Finally, I know in and for all things, we must give God praise.

LONG STORY FICTION

**Life journeys reflected in
this fictional long story.**

"As a fiction writer I am not always sure where reality ends and non reality begins, when sane thoughts become less than sane, or what is imagination versus undiscovered truth, but ultimately, it is my job to make you as unsure as I am."[5]
— Kathryn Mattingly, Benjamin

---

[5] www.goodreads.com/quotes/truth vs. fiction. Accessed November 14, 2023.

When The Vow Breaks
By Lillian Collins

Mercedes was 48, recently divorced, and her comfortable, unassuming life was about to change. Her ex-husband Lonnie acted like a spoiled teenager who was expected to keep his room clean. He got away without paying child support, even though he made well over six figures. Mercedes was determined to care for her son Robert, who recently was accepted at Morehouse. She kept telling herself that both of them would get through this "hurdle in the road."

Mercedes thought she would never marry again or meet anyone who would give her the lifestyle she had with Lonnie. Not only did she live in the big house in the suburbs, but she also flew to New York for Broadway shows and ate at Sardi's Restaurant. It was commonplace for them to see the Detroit Pistons and Chicago Bulls play in Detroit. They had floor seats and could almost reach out and touch the players; Bill Price and Joel Long.

Mercedes seemed to have it all; however, Lonnie was bipolar. Lonnie was 5 feet 5 inches tall and had a Napoleon

Complex. Someone rumored that he threatened to throw his boss out the window of his high-rise office. No one messed with Lonnie Harris. He was an advertising salesperson, bringing in a lot of revenue for CBS and NBC. He "wined and dined" with the advertising agencies, giving him all the business he never had to work for. That is how Mercedes and sometimes Robert got to enjoy the fringe benefits.

Mercedes and Lonnie were from Pittsburgh, a steel town, but they knew early on that Pittsburgh would not be their final destination. Soon after marriage, they transferred to Farmington Hills, Michigan. Farmington Hills had excellent schools and the average income in the 70s was sixty-thousand dollars a year.

They purchased their first home for fifty-seven thousand dollars. It was a neat three-bedroom, two-bath home in an all-white neighborhood. This did not bother them, because, in Lonnie's line of work, there were very few blacks; so they assimilated and made it work. They sent Robert to Red Bell pre-school, and Mercedes got a job with Hewlett Packard. They remodeled their home and purchased all new furniture. They were moving up in life.

One point to mention is that when Mercedes married Lonnie at twenty-five in 1967, she had five thousand dollars in savings and no debt. Being naïve and in love, she never asked about his personal life. Lonnie promised her that if she married him, she would live a glorious life because he had dreams.

After their marriage, Mercedes discovered Lonnie had a ton of debt, and his car was not drivable. Imagine the shock on Mercedes' face after marriage when the bill collectors started calling. She had never experienced this because she always paid her bills on time.

Thanks to Mercedes' mother, when she purchased her car at twenty years old, her mother took her to Mellon Bank. Mercedes borrowed her own money to purchase her car. When the car was paid off, the original principal was back in her bank account. She had a smart mother who only went to the seventh grade. Mercedes's mother worked for rich Jewish people and listened to them discussing finance and learned how to save.

Detroit turned out to be great for Mercedes and Lonnie. They were young and happy. Even though Lonnie had personality issues, things were going well for them. Mercedes's job was good, and she loved working at Hewlett-Packard.

Mercedes met some great folks at HP. She especially liked one engineer. He was 6 feet tall, with a gorgeous smile. He was tall, dark, and handsome. Their eyes met and something in Mercedes made her tingle all over.

Oliver came over and introduced himself to Mercedes, and she melted. When they saw each other, they would just smile. Mercedes did not see a ring on his finger, but she had a carat diamond on her left, third finger. He would flirt when his brown eyes met hers.

Mercedes knew her wardrobe was cool. When you work for a tech company, you wear brown khaki pants, a trendy t-shirt, and loafers. You looked like you were in a prep school and Fridays were always jeans and tennis shoes. One Friday, everyone was going out for lunch. Oliver asked Mercedes if she would like to ride with him and two others. Mercedes felt no harm. She consented to ride with him.

Oliver had a nice company car, Taurus, and she sat in the front. She noticed how cool he was, and his after-shave smelled expensive. He offered to pay for Mercedes's lunch, but Mercedes told him she had it. Oliver insisted on paying, so she gave up and accepted. He had arranged for the other two people to ride back with some other employees on their team. Mercedes felt a little uncomfortable, but knew it would be fine. The two of them talked and when they got back to the office, Oliver said they should do lunch again. Mercedes said "yeah." She enjoyed herself.

Hewlett Packard was to have an end-of-the-year holiday party, and you could not bring your spouse. Even though it was a lie, she told Lonnie that it was mandatory. She had to go to the party. There was a live band, food, and drinks. Her team was sitting together, and Oliver looked right at her when he strolled in with a couple of guys. She felt uncomfortable again because she was married. He walked over and took her hand; they danced most of the night.

Lonnie was always out late almost every night because he had to take the advertising execs out; so Mercedes knew this was part of his job. She also knew where to draw the line with Oliver.

Oliver was recently divorced, and she felt she could handle it. However, there was some trouble at home for her. Lonnie spent too much money, and she paid the bills. Lonnie was making $75K and Mercedes was making 24K.

That was still a lot of money for two people and one child in the 70s.

Lonnie spent all of Mercedes' savings. If she had listened to her mother, she would have left her money with her mother for safekeeping. Mercedes's father had died two years before she got married. So, her father never met Lonnie. But her mother felt he was not the right person for Mercedes.

Lonnie was an atheist which turned off Mercedes's mom. She had raised Mercedes in the church and taught her to put God first. Mercedes knew Lonnie was an atheist, but he was also a salesperson. He reminded her how hypocritical her church members were, and she agreed.

Oliver, Oliver, Oliver is all Mercedes could think about. They started meeting for lunch often. Oliver acted like he had feelings for Mercedes. She had feelings for him. Was Mercedes going to throw away her marriage for this man who had been divorced twice?

Mercedes came home from the holiday party to find out that Lonnie was promoted to district manager in Chicago. They had to move again. Mercedes had to quit HP and find another job in Chicago. The one person she would miss was

Oliver. She often wondered if she had stayed in Detroit, would her life have changed?

There was so much chemistry between the two of them. Every time she saw Oliver, her eyes would light up. They never kissed, but they flirted with each other, making Mercedes feel like she could have broken her vows. Interestingly enough, Lonnie physically broke the vows when he had an affair with Irena in Chicago.

SHORT STORIES NON-FICTION

Life journeys told in true short stories.

"Though nobody can go back and make a new beginning...
Anyone can start over and make a new ending."[6]
— Chico Xavier

---

[6] www.goodreads.com/quotes/life lessons. Accessed November 7, 2023.

Be Careful with Your Words

By Patricia Ann Callahan Morris

When growing into relationships, first, build a strong friend relationship by knowing what each enjoys. Talk about what you want in a relationship beyond what that person looks like, their education, financial status, morals, and ethics, their family relationships, their love of self before they love others. These are the basics of getting into a relationship.

Look for sincerity, empathy, and kindness. Do their words and actions fit with their efforts to understand what the person is saying? It is essential to know if the person wants a family or a career. Both must want that relationship to be a lifetime commitment, and not a temporary affair, where they intend to move on later.

It is essential to bring into the relationship what bothers them about each other. This helps to prevent severely crushed feelings, undue hurt and negative reactions toward things that just need to be discussed by them both.

I listened to a young man discussing a relation-ship; the young lady talked about how she was raised strictly and kept things from them because she felt they would be so opinionated in what she would tell them she thought about. It shut her down from sharing; she didn't want that when she had a child. The young man opened up about his dad's never-untiring relationships; he would berate them about having difficulty with math.

The father told him, "If you were on the side of the road begging for change, I would not stop to give you any." His father's words chopped his heart to pieces. The fear of becoming like his father terrified him and brought both of them to tears.

It was good that he could share that fear with her while considering growing closer to each other. It is important not to come into relationships with secrets.

We might not know everything about someone, but at least knowing some things helps to build the relationship. It is worth all the difficulties to become stronger and closer.

Those hurtful words of his father stayed with him all his life. He vowed to himself to never have a child and say that to them. Even subtle negative statements can wound them like a dagger. So be careful with your comments.

The young lady he was interested in said, "My parents were so strict I never told them what I was thinking because they were so opinionated about what I had to say about anything."

We must be careful of our words. In developing friendships or relationships of any type, you should always desire for people to see you as a quality man or woman. Then you should want that person to be someone you two together will try always to inspire each other to be the best persons you can be.

A Strong Black Woman
By Patricia Ann Callahan Morris

I look back on the history of strong women who embody courage, reliance, determination, independence, and confidence in themselves and their abilities, facing challenges head-on with grace and perseverance. I want to share the accolades I have observed on my life's journey regarding all strong black women.

So, sit back in your favorite chair and sip your coffee while I unveil a strong black woman in my life.

My mother's confidence in her capabilities to make hard decisions that aligned with her values and goals in our home and father's business was the building block I saw of a strong black woman. She could bounce back from setbacks and learn from her failures, make necessary changes, and grow from every situation ever stronger.

She taught my sister and me these strategies early in life. We will experience failure, but it is the foundation for learning to succeed and developing independence. She taught my sister and me that making excuses wasn't acceptable in our home and not allow others to define what we could or could not achieve.

Mother's empathy and compassion were extraordinary; supporting others and lifting their spirits were admirable in advocating for others' needs. A quality everyone who knew her expressed that same quality about her, even today.

Her communication skills in personal and professional leadership were an encouragement to make dreams work. I watched her captivating her audience. My sister and I were filled with pride.

The authenticity of my mom's uniqueness, celebrating her strength and embracing her imperfections, and unapologetically encouraging others to do the same. The power of women can manifest differently with every woman's journey.

A Student Stood Up To Adversity
By Patricia Ann Callahan Morris

A Student Stood Up and Faced Adversity with Dignity.

In 2023, I heard how an administrator of an institution behaved when corrected by a female African–American student about the reason for *Juneteenth*. It saddened me.

The student intended to share the importance of *Juneteenth*-a federal holiday, and what it meant to the African American communities. The Emancipation Proclamation, signed on June 19, 1865, declared the freedom of enslaved Black people in the United States.

The student received strict demands imposed on her to correct the institution's director for the real reason behind the *Juneteenth* celebration. The administrator kicked the student out of the school and threatened to have the police call to remove her from the premises if she didn't leave. The institution director did not realize the consequence of her action because she misunderstood the importance of the celebration of *Juneteenth*.

Despite threats of school expulsion and police intervention, the student's unwavering assertive-ness helped her to prevail through the power of the negative adversity. Even today, it is sad not to understand the significance of *Juneteenth* as a federal holiday on June 19th, 2023. There is reason to celebrate the freedom of Blacks from slavery in the United States, which was ended by the Emancipation Proclamation, signed on June 19th, 1885. That legally was supposed to end the enslavement of the Black people.

An institution's director didn't like the student's feedback that went viral about what she said in the classroom. Why can't we African-Americans recognize and celebrate *Juneteenth* as a federal holiday which intends to commemorate freedom without hate?

Sadly, today we continue to fight for that same freedom. That legally declared freedom was supposed to show our younger generations what and why our ancestors historically worked and died. That commitment to our freedom is a hundred and fifty-six years, from June 19th, 1885, to June 19th, 2023.

The signing in 2021 into law *Juneteenth* became a federal holiday day after Martin Luther King Jr. Day. There are corporations and other businesses that recognize *Juneteenth* as a paid day off, and others a day off without pay.

Final Weeks Tribute

By Denise Vick

My mother was a sharp-dressing-on-the-go older lady. Nothing stopped her, except for the following facts.

Her final weeks were filled with five hospital stays, one live-in rehabilitation facility, and one hospice center, which is where she took her final breath.

Because she was eighty-six no attorney was willing to take her case. Twenty-six or eighty-six, when a medical error is the cause, age should not be a factor. Now, it is proper that the fine or dollar amount at judgement weigh differently, but no accountability for actions or negligence. No! Age should not weigh in.

Far too many women die each year for lack of this simple yet deadly oversight. I know by now you want me to *cut to the chase*. Here it is; A Urinary Tract Infection (UTI). Yes, this common but deadly infection which claims the lives of far too many women each year. It added another name to its list on June 15, 2023.

How to stop it? A simple blood test for this all-too-common killer. It becomes septic and like many ladies, including my mother, destroys the vital organs. Thus, it causes a slow painful and weak death.

This was one ride my mother did not want to take. We had future plans laid out. This not only killed my mom, but my intended plans right out from under my feet.

The following poem, A Mother's Love, flowed from Denise after composing the story of her mother's preventable death. With an overflow of raw feelings, poetry flowed.

A Mother's Love

By Denise Vick

Never ending love.
Regardless of what you do or say,
through pain and sorrow,
Mother still loves you.

A mother's love
can bear the weight
of thousands of pounds' worth of
Letdowns, heartbreaks and even "Hate You's."

No matter how toxic you become.
Regardless of the many acidic burns.
A true mother continues to love.
You are her gift from God.

A mother's love is second only
to Jesus' love for us.
There should be no hatred,
even when you have to "let go and let God."

A mother's love
is always prayerful,
constantly hopeful,
never-ending.

A mother's love,
is fueled by faith,
moved by the Holy Ghost,
sustained by Jesus Christ.

I Am Proud Of Myself

By Patricia Ann Callahan Morris

I remember sitting quietly in my bedroom and dreaming about all I wanted to become, including a teacher like my aunts, and my dad a carpenter. I wanted them all to be proud of me.

My mom, the "powerhouse" resource who ran my father's company's business and our home, encouraged me to be what I wanted, but to be the best I could at it.

She reassured me I could be anything I wanted to become through hard work, determination, accountability, trustworthiness, and kindness, but not allowing others to believe those accolades were my weaknesses.

Every time I accomplished something, she said, "Your reputation will precede you." I didn't quite understand what that phrase meant as a child or teenager, but implanted it in my heart and continue to live by it.

Mom simply said, "A person may have never met you, but they already know all about you from the opinions of others that have heard." Keeping that in mind, throughout my life, it became fundamental to me.

That phrase always seems to resonate over and over in my mind when setting goals for work settings, at home, as a team player working on projects, teaching sons and students, as an adjunct professor, nieces and nephews, children in the neighborhood, and my grandchildren.

It still resonates strongly in my mind every day. Yes. I have made mistakes, but tried to learn from them and not repeat.

I am proud of myself for embracing life as a physical medicine practitioner for forty-three years, then I retired. I was a leader, a time manager, a listener, was respectful of others' opinions, even those that may have differed from my own. I continue to be all of these, while still being a Christian motivator, and a genuine friend.

Are you proud of yourself?

Have You Heard About Rahab?
By Trudie V. Lee

(See Joshua Chapters 2 and 6, KJV, and Mathew Chapter 1, KJV)

I would like to keep you in the loop. This is not gossip. This is not to be kept between you and me. You can share it. You must share it because everyone needs to know. Just tell the truth.

Have you heard about Rahab? First, you know Rahab was a harlot. Many looked at her as a plain old prostitute. There was nothing plain or old about Rahab.

She was a smart entrepreneur who owned and operated a business. Yes, she was beautiful, sexy, and captivating. But many looked upon her profession with contempt. Disgraceful, they thought. Though, their opinions didn't bother Rahab. She had a mind of her own. And that was the way she lived. She took care of her family and her business.

Rahab was a leader. She was competent, fearless and wise; known to be shrewd. She operated her business with skill, experience, and wisdom. Apparently, she was a keen listener and one who stored and kept secrets. Although some ignored her, ashamed of her fame, she has been talked about for centuries. Rahab possessed qualities that would take hours to discuss.

Rahab's is first seen in the Bible where Joshua sent out two spies to survey the enemy's country, Jericho. They went to Rahab's house to hide out. Spies are known to be highly intelligent. They are highly developed with mental and physical discipline. They are loyal and wholly committed. Joshua's spies were no different.

Joshua chose his best men to go out and spy on Jericho. They were on a serious mission. War was about to erupt. Maybe they questioned among themselves, *"What are we doing here?"* But they also knew within this challenge was a divine mission!

The spies did not question their intuition. They followed their inner leader. After speaking with Rahab, they knew they were in the right place at the right time. GOD had given them the "hook up."

Was Rahab chosen? Did she have a vision? Did GOD speak to her in a dream? Who revealed to her that, "…for the LORD your God, he is the God in heaven above, and in the earth beneath." (Joshua 2:11, KJV) Who gave her the courage to show favor to the spies—to commit treason against her king and country?

Oh, what courage! Rahab hid the spies from the king's officers. If caught, she and her entire family would have been killed. But what GOD ordained could not be stopped.

The spies and Rahab made an agreement. Strangers of different cultures and beliefs! Strangers brought together by GOD. Both kept their word. And both were saved.

Rahab changed her beliefs. She changed her culture. She married Salmon, an Israelite. They had a son named Boaz, and Rahab became an ancestor of JESUS!

There have been discussions for generations about the role of women in history and the role of women in today's society. GOD chose Rahab, regardless of her profession or status in society. GOD used her!

Question: Why would GOD choose a harlot, a prostitute, for such an important role?

Answer: GOD is GOD. HE is Sovereign. HE chooses whomever HE pleases.

No Time To Waste

By Patricia Ann Callahan Morris

As I age, my time is valuable to me. I would rather not spend my time on anything unproductive.

I view time in three phases shared by a former client's husband from Europe. His rendition of time captivated me. I have embraced it as my chronological barometer.

In the first phase of time, I *Anticipate* what I believe will happen, but do not truly understand the "ins and outs" of wasting time. I call it *fantasizing* about what I want to happen. I switch back and forth between what I want and do not want. But time doesn't stop. It keeps ticking. *TikTok, TikTok,* on and on. During this time I feel I wasted two years' time.

In the second time phase, I experience *Realization*. As I age, I must take responsibility for my life and plan for my goals, making better decisions for myself *and* my son's future. *TikTok, TikTok.* Time waits for no one.

The last phase of time is my *Memories*. I replay my childhood play, friends, and classmates. I recall my marriages, divorces, giving birth, and working. I reminisce about traveling, laughing, and enjoying family. Friends, visits, and events; all flash before my mind's eye. In this phase, my blessings and grace bring to me memories of joy and even sadness, as I recall those who were my special treasures. Those treasures were always a wonderful benefit in my thought time.

So, I beg of you, don't waste your time on something that you feel wastes your time, *TikTok, TikTok.* Time waits for no one.

We Take It For Granted

By Patricia Ann Callahan Morris

We Take It for Granted refers to the unfortunate tendency of individuals to not fully appreciate or value the things they have in their lives. Today, a Christian mission group shared their experiences in a remote village in Jamaica.

The Snellville Christian Church mission group comprised males and females, adults, and three teenagers. Listening to their stories, I couldn't help but reflect on things we take for granted. The group's experiences highlighted the stark differences in lifestyle between America and the remote village they visited.

That Jamaican village lacked the bare necessities of life. For instance, mental health services are an unaffordable luxury. Hearing about parents who took their loved ones to in-house mental health facilities because they couldn't afford to care for they and themselves was heart-wrenching.

The group also shared stories about the food they ate in the village. A peanut butter sandwich was their option. Pastor Dale was on a mission to find a burger, which was a treat, and he found it. Everyone in the group knows a burger is one of his favorites. The group appreciated having options at home, but the people in the village did not have the same options.

The work ethic of the people in the village was inspiring to the mission group. Despite the sweltering conditions of both heat and humidity, the men and women worked tirelessly without the aid of air conditioning. They endured all the demands heat placed on them.

The contractor and the other males carried loads of ninety pounds on their shoulders up the steep hill to build a chicken house. It was an amazing work ethic to be observed by the mission group.

The mission group worked hard to prepare the school for the students. They built a bob-wired fence, made a concrete ramp, and painted the interior and external of the school. The two women in the group exchanged anecdotes, revealing their talents in hand-making curtains out of towels for the classroom window. Overall, the group's experiences showed their passion, love, and respect for the people of the village.

With limited sign language knowledge, one of the mission men formed a bond with a young male in the village, bringing joy to the boy who felt cared for. It was a reminder not to take things for granted. It's essential to be resourceful and appreciate what we have, even if it could be better.

We can learn from those who have less to improve things. Let's stop taking it for granted and start appreciating the blessings in our lives.

The village people showed their faith in God. They stayed grounded in faith, grounded in gratitude, and grounded in obedience. We can learn from those with so much less. We need to stop taking our blessings for granted and start appreciating more of the good things we have in our lives.

Prayer For Healing
By Tjuana Ladawn Callahan

Father God, I Thank You for this morning. Thank You for life, health, and strength. I will enter Your gates with thanksgiving and Your courts with praise! You are worthy of all honor, all glory, and all praise! I will bless You, oh Lord, at all times. Your praise shall continually be in my mouth. My soul will boast in You. Surely, there is nothing too hard for You.

Forgive me for my sins. I have not been trusting You fully. I have been impatient. I have been busy, busy, busy. I think if I'm not doing something, nothing will get done. I have been trying to work *for* You (in placed of You) instead of allowing You to work *through* me and in me.

My life is out of order. My home is a wreck. I continue to neglect home while doing, doing, doing for others. I know You want me to help others. But You also want me to take care of the home You have given me. Help me get in order. I need You.

Father, forgive me for losing faith in Your healing power. Your dear child has been in the ICU for one month and it seems like little progress has been made. But that's because I'm looking through my eyes. You know best. You are in control, no matter what it looks like to me. Her life is in Your hands. You are the Alpha and the Omega—the Beginning and the Ending. You are Jehovah Rapha, the God who heals. You are the Creator and Redeemer.

You are able to do exceedingly abundantly above all we dare ask or even think according to the power that works in us through Jesus the Christ. So, I say, let Your will be done and not my own. Your will and Your way are perfect. So, I ask, what is Your purpose in this experience of her illness and hospital say? What am I to learn? What are we to learn? Teach us Your will and Your way concerning this experience.

Thank You for continuing to give the medical staff caring for her the wisdom and insight to do what's best. Touch Your dear child with Your finger of love, peace, mercy, goodness, kindness, meekness, faithfulness, joy, and self-control.

God, we know you can heal. And so, I Thank You for healing in the way that you will. Your dear child confessed Jesus as her Lord and Savior. She is Your child first. We have the blessed assurance of knowing that Your daughter is etched in the palm of Your hand. Therefore, she cannot be plucked out. You are her Savior and Redeemer. You are with her now and unto the end—even throughout eternity.

Holy Spirit, speak to my heart. I am listening. Speak to all our loved ones. Make Your message truly clear in a way that each one of us will understand at our varied levels of understanding. Then Father, we must accept Your word, Your truth, Your will, Your teaching, Your guidance, Your perfecting in us. Your wisdom is perfect.

Surely, You are greater than this situation. You are Almighty, Omnipotent, Omniscient, and Omnipresent. You are Sovereign. I yield myself to You. Create in me a clean heart, oh God, and renew a right spirit within me. I submit my body to You as a living sacrifice, holy acceptable to You. This is my reasonable service. I will not be conformed to this world, but I will be transformed by the renewing of my mind to prove what is that good, perfect, and acceptable will You have purposed in my life.

I want to walk worthy of the calling You have in my life. I need You. We need You, Father God. Thank You for being our Shield and our Strong Tower. We rest in You. By faith,

I am focused and trusting You. I love You Lord Jesus. AMEN

My Mom Is Still In The House

By Patricia Ann Callahan Morris

Our home situations have changed over the years. Now more than ever in the history of humanity, our morals and ethics are missing and need to be reinstated. There is no required posted expiration date.

Mom is gone. But Mom's spirit is still in the house. I hear her whisper words of wisdom when I am troubled. I know Mom is still in the house.

Mom was present when we kneeled to say our prayers as we repeated, "Now, I lay me down to sleep. If I die before I wake, I pray the Lord my soul to keep." I am now an adult. My prayer has changed, "Giving us this day our daily bread." Daily bread spiritually provides all we need in food, shelter, and health, all for keeping our faith in Him in this house. Mom is still in the house.

Her spirit and words linger throughout this house with her wisdom, protection, and love for us. My mom is still in the house.

Sipping Sufficient Grace
"God turned the water into gasoline"
By Donna J. Ware

Excerpted from my unpublished, incomplete work –
Sipping From Saucers

The old-timey, Biblical miracle, in fact Jesus' first miracle, was when He turned the water into fine wine at a wedding, at His mother's request. Although He knew it was not yet His time to perform wonders, He did it to please His mom.

A modern-day miracle, in fact one so mind-boggling that it still brings tears of joy to my eyes and tingles all over my body, is the one about my dad, no money, a vehicle full of his family and saints of God, and an empty gas tank far from home, with just God to lean upon.

Dad pulled up to the gas tank, weary from the long day, full of joy because of the blessed church service. Dad's pockets held only pennies. He knew he did not have enough pennies to make it on home. His kids were in the car. What was he going to do? But before he could allow worry to creep in, God spoke to him.

God told my dad to go over there to the right by that water spigot and get that empty gas can and fill it full of water. This reminds me of the widow and the pots, and shutting the door so no one would ask what a crazy thing she was doing. They did not realize the miracle God was about to work in her life, filling all of those vessels full of valuable oil she sold and could live off of the rest of her life. Even more miraculous, just like God made the oil flow from heaven, He shut it off when her last vessel was full.

Now, back to my dad. He never said a word to any of us. He just filled the can full of water and took it to our gas tank and poured it in. He did it believing. He did it because he recognized the voice of God. He did it because there was "no other help he knew." He had stepped out there on a "wing and a prayer."

Dad had to trust God. And like a baby who has blind faith to believe the parents will take care of their needs, Dad had to believe like a little child that God was not going to leave us stranded so far from home after sacrificing so much to get to the service to worship Him.

So with his measure of blind faith, Dad did as God told him and our car drank that water. It was miraculously and immediately transformed from water out of the spigot into the proper gasoline our vehicle needed. Dad drove us home and drove on that miraculous tank of gasoline the entire week to and from his job until Friday's paycheck time. This was all by God's goodness, mercy, and grace, and my dad's trust in the Lord.

Sometimes, our backs are against the wall. We have no other option but to trust God or fail. That choice is always ours to make. God cares for those who love Him. He promises in His Word to never leave or forsake us. (See Deuteronomy 31:16) He wants you, dear reader, and the world to know that He is still in the miracle and wonder-working business.

To God be all the glory.

Secret

By Patricia Ann Callahan Morris

Parents, please take time to have conversations with their children to prevent them from keeping secrets that could save their lives. It should exclude no topic. Allow them to share their concerns with someone who has their best interests at heart.

A little girl kept from her parents a secret. She was to go play with the neighboring friend's daughter, Mary Ann Davis. While waiting, she bounced her red ball, awaiting her best friend.

The day was sunny, and a light breeze blew in her long hair as she bounced the bright-colored ball on the sidewalk. She counted one, two, three, and so on. A tall, good-looking man approached her and spoke. "Hi," and she kept on bouncing her ball. She thought he was a polite passerby.

Then he asked her, "Can you tell me where the nearest drugstore is located? I am new around here?" She stopped bouncing the ball and said, "Sir. Hastings Street." He says, "Can you show me, and I will buy you an ice cream cone? What flavor do you like?" The little girl says, "Vanilla." As a seven-year-old child, she does not know of the danger of this man's intent.

They both walked down the street, and he held her hand. Then someone from a house called out to him, "Who is the pretty little girl?" His reply was, "She is my niece, man." The little girl did not realize that he had just moved into the neighborhood. He should know no one.

They stopped further down the block, and he said, "This is where I live, and I need to get more money so I can buy you that ice cream cone. I promised you." They entered a building with a large glass door, opened it, went inside, and started down a darkened stairway until a loud voice yelled, "What are doing here?"

Why?

By Patricia Ann Callahan Morris

As a small child into adulthood, I have always wanted to know the "Why?" about something. I have been passionate about knowing the "Why?" and not accepting what someone tells me as a fact or simply what they believe. I like to start by asking the "Why.?"

Why wait to say everything about someone we love until they are gone? Why do we delay doing things for someone until it is too late to do it? Why wait for someone else to do something and then say I plan to do that? Why can't we accept our mistakes rather than make excuses? Why promise something you had no intention of doing in the first place?

Why accept mis-justice and say it is the status quo? Why stand around and watch others do and criticize? Why not shut your mouth and not show others what a big fool you can make of yourself?

Why not give gifts and flowers when the person can enjoy and smell the flowers? Why blame your spouse? Why didn't you do things differently in your relationship? Why give up your faith when things are going back for you? Why do you say, "I have not?" Let us be humble and grateful for what we have.

115

Self-Worth

By Patricia Ann Callahan Morris

Defining your self-worth requires self-evaluation of one's feelings of their own self. Believing you deserve better things, that you are a good person, and you have something to give back to others.

Self-worth is the confidence to defend your values to others, allowing you to believe in yourself and not allowing others to define your worthiness. During our lifetimes, it requires looking back and reassessing our dignity in careers, work-settings, relationships, friendships, family obligations, and to look ahead to our future endeavors aiming to maintain the highest self-esteem.

My mother used to say, "What are we doing here?" It was her way of reassessing her self-worth as a black woman, wife, mother, friend, and businesswoman and her interactions with the customers in my father's company. I observed her precise decision-making in important company transactions. In-person she displayed excellence in communication and documentation. She set a high bar for my sister and me to follow. To her, realizing failure was the means to personal learning growth and guidance toward success.

A Disciplined Prayer Life
By Donna J. Ware

You must make time for prayer. With God's intervention and your commitment to pray every day, God can make the hours of your day accommodate your daily time with Him. Your time could be minutes, or it could be hours every day. Your prayer time may have to be very early in the morning, or it might have to be en route to work. This may be your only time for yourself that you feel you can commit with conviction to spend with God. Many families have spoken of spending their commute time praying.

Your time may be in the shower, or quiet time in your special prayer "closet," or at your desk when you first get to work, or during your break or lunchtime. You may be a "night owl" whose mind comes alive in the wee hours of the morning, like me. This is also a perfectly good time to commune with God. The Almighty God never slumbers or sleeps (See Psalm 121) so any time is a good time to God. The world does not always offer ideal situations, but that is what discipline is all about—making it work for you; finding the time and committing to it daily.

The "where" is not so important either, but that you do pray is imperative. Create a habit of going into prayer at the same time of each day (if at all possible). Daily prayer is a Christian discipline.

Pray for yourself, so you can be a better disciple to others; pray for others, so they can be blessed and be a blessing to others; pray for the government; pray for the world; pray for the healing of Jerusalem as it says in Psalm 122:6, Pray for the peace of Jerusalem: *"May those who love you be secure."* (NIV) Although you can say much in your prayers, remember *"Thy will be done"* is all that has to be said about each of your requests. You are then entrusting God's perfect will to be perfected in yourself, in others, and the world.

Years ago, renowned authoress and spokeswoman Evelyn Christensen wrote the book, *What Happens When Women Pray*[7]. This book opened my eyes to the power behind a disciplined prayer life, and in the power of many praying at the same time on one accord. Sometimes God allows us to pray an extraordinarily long time for a situation, salvation, or

---

[7] Evelyn Christensen. What Happens When Women Pray. Deluxe ed. Chapter Four. Colorado Springs: David C. Cook, 1975.

healing of someone.

When this happens, do not give up. Just keep praying and checking. Check to be certain your motives are godly, not selfish, and are solely for the glory of God. Pray, pray, and keep on praying until the change comes. Your prayer should offer praise to God first. Then you present your petition - what you need God to do for you. Then once again, you give Him thanks and praise.

From that prayer forward, if your request is not answered immediately, realize God is not hard of hearing. He knows your request, now walk in trusting confidence and give Him praise. Trust His will, His ways and His timing. Until the change comes, continue to give Him praise.

Several things can happen when your prayers are not immediately answered,

1. You are being tested to see just how faithful you are and how deeply your trust in the Lord has grown.

2. God can be testing your motives—all prayer requests must be for God's glory, His purpose and His will.

3. God's ways, thoughts and timing are not like yours— you have to trust Him completely.

The Word states, *"Devote yourselves to prayer, being watchful and thankful."* (Colossians 4:2, NIV) And in the 100th Psalm it says to, *"Enter into his gates with thanksgiving, and into his courts with praise: be thankful unto him, and bless his name."* (vs. 4, NIV) This may seem overwhelming during the more turbulent spiritual youth level years and other times, but God is faithful and just. He will help see you through.

My Family Reunion

By Patricia Ann Callahan Morris

Family reunions hold significant importance in my family for cultural and social reasons. Planning and organizing a successful family reunion was a challenge that required coordinating schedules, choosing a suitable location, and deciding on activities that catered to the older adults and the young people and their interests.

My grandmother was the person the family sought to coordinate for our family union. My uncles, aunts, nieces, and nephews were all delegated to do specific tasks. They met at Grandmama's home and planned to meet her before the formal announcement to our family in various states.

During our gatherings in a large yard, were tables with white cloths draping them and wooden chairs set all around for the older adults. The tables and chairs for the younger folks, were covered with plaid red and white tablecloths

In the center of the big yard was a large, long wooden table dressed with a bright white tablecloth loaded with an assortment of meats, salads, vegetables, pies, cakes and cookies, beverages, cups, plates, napkins, and utensils were conveniently placed at the end of the table. I can still envision foods and their aromas as a young girl. Our family reunion with my parents and sister going to visit from the North..

Grandma and the ladies wore white aprons with white towels hanging from the apron pocket and prepared the table with more and more food until you could hardly see the tablecloth underneath.

Before the food was served, Pastor Jenkins and his family were invited. He said the blessing. All we young people hoped the pastor would not be long-winded because we were ready to eat. The line formed first with the older adults, and the servers placed food on their plates, and then the younger people we lined up for the servers to serve us. Grandmama had everything organized for this special occasion.

After the meal, the activities took place on the other side of the yard for the kids. The older adults sat on the large front screened porch, talking and laughing. The younger people played games until Grandmama said for everyone to come inside.

Then the younger people sat on the floor around the fireplace. They listened to the storytelling of the older adults about their lives. They showed old family photos, while sharing words of wisdom, telling jokes, and making everyone laugh.

This was the best time for me besides eating good food. I took photos with my Brownie Hawkeye Camera with a large flash which almost blinded the older adults when it flashed. I tried to take candid shots of the family reunion for our memories and to share later. I sent copies of those photos to Grandmama.

Family reunions have been different since the passing of Grandmama. Everyone's schedule is too busy for some odd reasons. It will always be different with her gone. Our reunions are now planned differently than in the past.

Soul Testing
by Donna J. Ware

I could have titled these thoughts—Joy Testing, but as I dwelled on the facts, I realized it is the soul that is tested for joy, because joy springs up from the soul. The soul houses the mind, will, and emotions. Joy affects all three areas within the soul. Thus, I call this chat—Soul Testing.

The Bible says, *"When anxiety was great within me, your consolation brought joy to my soul."* (Psalm 94:19, NIV, 1984) You will be tested in the areas of joy. If you look to God, He will replace anxiety with His joy. Paul leaves you an exceptionally great example when he spoke from his prison cell, *"Rejoice in the Lord always: and again I say rejoice."* (Philippians 4:4, KJV)

He continues his teaching to the Philippians by saying, *"Not that I speak in respect of want: for I have learned, in whatsoever state I am, therewith to be content."* (Philippians 4:11, KJV)

The Book of Psalm says, *"But let all those that put their trust in thee rejoice: let them ever shout for joy, because thou defendest them: let them also that love thy name be joyful in thee.* (5:11, KJV)

In the Epistle of James, the Word speaks,

² My brethren, count it all joy when ye fall into divers temptations;

[3] Knowing this, that the trying of your faith worketh patience. (KJV)

You should be reassured by what the Word says in Nehemiah, *"… for the joy of the Lord is your strength."* (8:10b, KJV) Moreover, in 1 Peter 4:13 it says, *"But rejoice, inasmuch as ye are partakers of Christ's sufferings; that, when his glory shall be revealed, ye may be glad also with exceeding joy."* (KJV)

Dad (Willmore D. Goins) once told me you could always tell a *true Christian* by how he or she smiles in the midst of the worst ever possible storm of his or her life. He said, with all the problems life has to offer, we must "count it all joy."

To God be all the glory.[8]

---

[8] Donna J. Ware. Growing UP in God. Chapter Five, "Adulthood to Seniorhood in Christ." CreateSpace: TN, 72-73.

Women in Positions Once Held By Men

By Patricia Ann Callahan Morris

It is now common to see women occupying roles traditionally held by men. There was a time when we only saw women as homemakers, domestic workers, or lesser roles in the 18th century. The changes are entirely different in the 19th and 20th centuries.

Women have shown they are intellectually capable and proficient in the vast array of professions today, both here in the United States of America and in countries aboard.

We women are accomplished in diverse fields, including politics, medicine, education, judges, senators, vice-president, research, business CEOs, design, film, writing, singing, aviation, journalism, ministry, and engineering. Women's current contributions in a world dominated by men serve as an inspiration to women from the past who faced unequal opportunities and lack of respect while pursuing their goals. I think about it often. They persisted despite the challenges.

As a young girl, I remember being a student at Chadsey High School and wanting to study mechanical drafting and architecture. Those courses were surmised to be for male students only. I spoke with my parents about my wishes and hoped they would be supportive. My dad was a well-known builder in the community, and was my role model for learning about those two fields. I dreamed one day to work beside him in his office.

My parents consulted with my counselor, Mr. Dolittle, who initially hesitated since the class was all male. He said, "I must bring this up before Mr. Carol Christy, the Principal." My parents were satisfied with his decision to consider the request because I was a student with high academic grades.

Women will most likely continue to be strong in pursuing their dreams and aspirations, even working harder to show their exceptional knowledge for years and centuries to come. When we are given a gift from God, no man has the right to take away what God has given. It was my dream as a young woman to become not only a homemaker but to also have a career.

I salute women of the past, present, and future for becoming *whatever* as they were and are inspired to pursue their faith in God. He is always walking with us and holding our hands helping us to make our contributions to humanity.

LONG STORIES NON-FICTION

Life journeys told in these true long stories.

"Accept yourself, love yourself, and keep moving forward. If you want to fly, give up what weighs you down."[9] — Roy T. Bennett, *The Light in the Heart.*

---

[9] www.goodreads.com/quotes/life lessons. Accessed November 7, 2023.

Broken Glass

by Tjuana Ladawn Callahan

Journal entry—December 21st

Each morning, my sister and I begin with a morning prayer call at 6:30AM. We were praying for the miraculous glory of God—to see His power and glory by faith. After our prayer time, I continued reading and meditating on the scriptures.

> O God, you are my God; I earnestly search for you. My soul thirsts for you; my whole-body longs for you in this parched and weary land where there is no water. I have seen you in your sanctuary and gazed upon your power and glory. Your unfailing love is better than life itself; how I praise you! I will praise you as long as I live, lifting up my hands to you in prayer. (Psalm 63:1-4, NLT)

This is a Psalm of David while he was in the wilderness of Judah, praying and seeking God.

The Apostle Paul talks about the struggle of living in this flesh and his desire for spiritual strength. He said, "we walk by faith." (See 2 Corinthians 5:1-8, NKJV)

We read the miraculous account of Jesus saying to Martha about her deceased brother Lazarus, "if you believe, you will see the glory of God." (See John 11:38-44, NKJV)

After studying and meditating, I lay my head down and dozed off to sleep. It was a Saturday morning, and I had no immediate plans. It was very peaceful and quiet. Joy was still sleeping. I really do not know if I was half-sleep, half-awake, or fully sleep nor how long. Suddenly, I heard the smashing sound of breaking glass. It was very loud, startling me to consciousness. I sat straight up. I thought surely someone had broken a window. But aside from the breaking glass, I did not hear anything else.

So, I got up immediately and started looking through the house at all the windows. Seeing none broken, I began looking out of the windows. The neighborhood was motionless and silent. Then there's the basement. I feared the broken window could be in the basement. I dared not open the door to go down those steps. What should I do?

I grabbed my cell phone to call 911. I told the 911 dispatcher to send a police officer because I could not figure out where the breaking glass was. I need an officer to search the basement with me. I called to Joy, "Did you hear that?" She said, "Yes." But she did not move from her bed. Now, I was putting on my clothes and demanding, "Joy, get up and put on some clothes. The police are coming."

I looked out the window again and saw my neighbor in his driveway talking on the phone. My thoughts were, "oh no," I do not want the police to come without him understanding what was going on. I was about to go out the door when Joy stopped me. Mom, she said, look, this is the broken glass. She was pointing to a picture frame that fell off of the wall and shattered into pieces on the floor. The wooden frame to the side of the glass and the framed content.

WHAT! This was the breaking glass that sounded like an intruder invading my home. Oh no, I called 911. I walked out the door to call 911 again and cancel my request. I was still concerned about my neighbor standing in his driveway talking on his cell phone. What if the police came for no reason at all? I thought. That would be a waste of his time. I explained to the 911 dispatcher that I wanted to cancel because I discovered where the broken glass was. I didn't want to tell her what it was, but she asked the question. Finally, I said it was a picture frame that fell on the living room floor. It seemed so trivial that I had been so alarmed by a fallen picture frame. The dispatcher canceled the request, and the conversation ended.

Standing in the driveway, I got my neighbor's attention and explained to him what had just happened. "I scared myself because of a picture frame that fell on the floor. I thought someone had broken into the house." He was empathetic. "In this day, in this season" he said, "burglary is happening everywhere." He was concerned about the same type of thing even though we live in a quiet neighborhood.

My next thought was to go back inside and clean up the glass. As I approached the picture frame and glass on the floor, I finally took a good look at it. It had been stationary on the wall for a long time. This was a framing of my first publication of poetry entitled, *Ain't God Good!* Mom purchased a copy and framed it. I hung it on the wall. That was 15 years ago. For all those years, this frame was taken down only for the painting of the walls.

What made it fall? My focus shifted—OK Father God— What are you saying to me? I wish this had been my first reaction before calling the police and getting all frantic, but it wasn't. Now I was faced with *Ain't God Good!* This was not just a picture falling. It was a message from God. I started to pick up the glass and stopped. I picked up my cell phone, accessed the camera, and started taking pictures of the sight on the floor just as it was. Then, I took pictures of the wall where the frame fell from.

The nail was secure in the wall. When satisfied that I captured the scene, I began picking up the glass. Now I could examine the frame, the book, the mounting, and the back of the frame. Oh—the mounting was cardboard backing which wore through tearing the mounting—causing the frame to fall. I took a picture of the mounting along with the frame front and back.

Wow! I was still thinking, what does this mean, Father? What are you saying? I don't think it was a chance occurrence. But my thoughts were interrupted. Joy had to go to work and needed me to take her. OK -OK Joy. I'm coming. I thought to myself, I will get back to this in peace when I return home.

On the way, we stopped at McDonald's, and I needed gas. We stopped at the corner for both. She went to McDonald's, and I went to the gas station. As I walked through the door to pay for the gas with $20 cash, a customer standing in line turned to me. "Whoa–Holy Spirit—Holy Spirit" he stated, looking at me. I replied, "Yes, Holy Spirit." I was very curious about the way he greeted me because he looked half drunk. But I continued listening and did not dismiss him.

I stood in my tracks for a moment at the door as he continued talking to me. He said, "You're a praying woman. Keep praying. It will happen by the Holy Spirit. Supernaturally—Miraculously." He continued talking while I moved toward the cashier for the gas. $15 on pump #2. Receiving $5 change from the purchase, I was ready to go. He had the nerve to ask me if I could spare any change. He went on to say, $5 would be nice. To that I replied, "I'm sure that it would be nice, but I was hungry myself and was going to get some breakfast. I was not giving him the $5."

As he spoke to me, I acknowledged the man, even though I was cautious. Who was this man and why was he talking to me? Is he for real? As I was saying, he kept talking to me about God's goodness. Once again, I was captivated—at a standstill. I don't remember everything he said because my mind was distracted by the appearance of the messenger. Finally, I said, "We're blocking the door. Walk with me to the car." Opening the door, he approached another woman who knew him, calling him by name. She hugged him and invited him back to church. She had a smile on her face, and they were happy to see each other.

As we continued walking and we approached the car, Joy was in the car waving me to "Come on." The messenger looked at Joy and said, "Prophet! She's a prophet. She's not ready yet. No, she's not ready yet." Joy was yelling, "Mama, come on and stop talking to that man." Speaking to Joy, he said, "Why are you afraid to preach?" To that Joy replied, "I'm not afraid to preach!" "That's my daughter," I said. Joy pulled out $1 and gave it to him. "Mama, get in the car. Let's go."

Now he directed his comments to me again, and I listened. I was intrigued and decided this could be an angel for all I know. Joy's retort was, "Get away! I'm calling 911." Be he stood his ground. I started getting in the car. He put his hand on my forehead and started praying. Joy became furious. She got out of the passenger seat and walked to the driver's side. "Get your hands off of my mama!" He finished his prayer and stepped back.

Joy walked back to the passenger seat. "Mama, let's go." I pulled away from the gas pump as I continued to her workplace less than 2 minutes away. I dropped her off and was ready to go immediately back home. I was contemplating, "What just happened?" At the first red light, I remembered that I didn't get the gas. I called Joy to fuss at her. "Joy, I didn't get the gas!" "Ah Mom," she replied, "just go back to the attendant. They will see that you didn't pump gas. Mom, hurry up."

I went back to the gas station, half hoping that I would see this angel again. Maybe I should have given him the $5. I wasn't hungry anymore. This time, I did not see him at the gas station at all. Just as Joy stated, the attendant in the store happily reset the pump. I apologized that I had been distracted. Pumping the gas—I saw no sign of this man anywhere. I decided I had indeed encountered an angel.

While driving back home, I tried to remember everything that was said. But I could not. The Mother of Jesus, Mary, came to mind. She said to the angel that visited her, "Be it unto me just as you say." I prayed this prayer:

Father, I don't know who that person was. But, if he was Your messenger, whatever truth he spoke to me—Be it unto me just as You say. I receive the truth of Your words. Be it unto me just as You say. Thank You. In Jesus' Name. Amen.

Forgive me for not giving him the $5. I'll place it in the offering place next time I go to church.

In meditation as I was driving, repeated all the way home. I am Your servant, Tjuana, be it unto me just as You say.

Finally, home, I immediately took off my coat and put on comfortable clothes. I was back in bed where I did my studying, meditating, and writing. I picked up the framed book, my journal, a pen, my Bible and rested against the headboard. Ain't God Good! OK Father, I'll write. What do you want me to write? I began to brainstorm everything that came to mind.

 It fell down.
Crash
Breaking glass
Suddenly
It was there all the time.
Miraculously
Supernaturally
Ain't God Good!
It's time to write.

I thought about the miraculous birth of Jesus Christ. I thought about Mary. The Holy Spirit reminded me of many things I heard in prayer and Bible study. The words I received on Thursday night, "Next year will be the Year of

Deliverance and Salvation." With all these thoughts, poetry began to flow from my mind to the pen.

Angels also visited the wise men and the shepherds.

The words of Jesus, "I am The Way, The Truth, and the Life."

Jesus came down to bring deliverance and salvation.

Jesus—God saves.

Jesus said, "He sent Me to heal the brokenhearted, to preach deliverance. . . ."

Deliverance Came Down!—That's IT! That's the title of the poem!

I continued writing until the poem was complete. Wow—God gave me a poem. I received deliverance and God delivered a poem. Praise You Father. I know when You give me poetry, people are blessed. It had been five years since God gave me a poem. Poetry used to flow through me freely. That was before divorce. In the marital struggle, so was my struggle to write. In the loss of divorce, was the loss of my desire to write.

My Pastor encouraged me to write through my struggles. He would say to me, "Tjuana, Ain't God Good?" I would say, "Yes, Pastor." He looked at me and I looked back with a distant look in my eyes. The divorce devastated me. Everything I had written in the past seemed to be a lie. I couldn't trust my thoughts. I could not—I would not yield my mind or my hands to write. These were the silent years. Family, friends, and acquaintances asked, "Have you been writing? When will your next book be out?" I could only give them a blank look. I haven't been writing; I don't know.

December 21ˢᵗ is so significant to me. God gave me another poem! I feel revived, renewed, and restored. Everyone who knows me, and my poetry is just as excited as I am. Ain't God Good! After sharing it with others, I began to study it. God speaks to me each time I read it, providing new revelation about the words He gave me:

The scripture references.

The deliverance call.

The King of Salvation.

Our Lord and Savior, Jesus Christ.

Thank You Holy Spirit.

AMEN.

Courageous Women Of African-American Descent

Patricia Ann Callahan Morris

The Courageous African American women have helped to seek equality for our people in politics, civil rights, literature, arts, science, education, and the military.

The quest for freedom was challenging in the early years, but I still know these eight women as forces that showed courage beyond one's imagination.

Ms. Sojourner Truth was born into slavery small in stature and is renowned for her activism in the abolitionist and women's rights movements. She was a vocal advocate for eradicating slavery and for the fight for women's suffrage in America.

Her famous speech is still inspiring, and rings out loudly, "Ain't I a woman?" She presented her well-known speech at Ohio's Woman's Convention in 1851, emphasizing race, class, gender, and the struggle for equality in a specific group.[10]

---

[10] *Sojourner Truth, 'Quest for Liberty and Justice, Dr. Nell Irvin Painter, Paul O'Neal, Esq.,* Thomas I Pully, October 2022 Schomburg Center for Research in Black Culture, The *New York Public Library.*

I respect *Harriet Tubman* as a woman resembling *Moses*. Harriet Tubman was a formerly enslaved person who became a prominent abolitionist and conductor of the Underground Railroad. Harriet's courage helped hundreds of slaves and her family out of slavery to freedom.

She carried a Winchester rifle while traveling through the dense woods. Ms. Tubman used stars to guide her along the dangerous route to North America and Canada.

I saw the historic Underground Railroad ten years ago, in Xenia, Ohio, down the road from my niece's home. It was a fantastic moment to remember Harriet Tubman as a brave woman who risked her life for her people's freedom, with the knowledge of God's presence by her side.[11]

An educator named *Mary Mc Leod Bethune* was born in the South. Mary Mc Lead Bethune was an educator and civil rights leader. She founded Bethune-Cookman University in Florida and was an advisor to President Franklin D. Roosevelt, advocating for African Americans' rights and women's empowerment.

My sister and I were told stories by my mother's sister, an educator about Ms. Bethune's contributions as a woman

---

[11] Harriet Tubman, Called Her Moses (2018), Full Movie, Dr. Eric Lewis Williams.

during summer vacation in the South. Upon our return to the North, my sister and I shared those riveting stories with our playmates on our schoolhouse backyard porch steps. They did not teach this knowledge in the late forties and fifties, in the schools in the North.[12]

Rosa Parks was born in the South. She was a crucial educator in the Civil Rights movement in the later fifties in Montgomery, Alabama. She sparked the Montgomery Bus Boycott, contributing significantly to the fight against segregation.

The Montgomery Bus Boycott shut down the bus services for extended periods while the women who worked in the white people's homes walked or rider-pooled to and from their homes. My father referred to it as changing our financial power against discrimination by the Montgomery Bus Company. Father said, "Hitting them in the pockets will bring the realization money talks, or we can continue to walk against discrimination."[13]

---

[12] Mary Mc Leod Bethune, National Council of Negro Women 7 Chapter, National Museum of African American History & Culture, Dayton's Education, and Industrial Training School for Negro Girls Annual Catalog (1910-2911).
[13] Rosa Parks, Telling Her Own Story at the Library of Congress in 2014, Howard G. Buffett, made a permanent gift in 2016 through the generosity of the Howard G. Buffett Foundation.

Maya Angelou was an influential poet, author, and civil rights activist. Maya's works, including her autobiography, "I Know Why the Caged Bird Sings," shed light on the African American experience; and inspired many people of color. When she spoke, she exuded the essence of a true woman. Her words resonated emotions beyond our expectations.[14]

Katherine Johnson was another brilliant woman as a mathematician and aerospace engineer. Ms. Johnson significantly contributed to the early U.S. Space Program, including trajectory calculations for NASA's moon landing mission. During her early days at NASA, she experienced both discrimination as a woman and as an African American.

Ms. Johnson had to leave the building to gain access to a "colored only" bathroom. Upon her return, her commander asked why she was late. During that time, the bathroom in her building was accessible only by white engineers. She talked about the race-based restriction of people of color, including herself, in the movie "Hidden Figures."[15]

Shirley Chisholm became the first African woman elected to the United States Congress. She was a vocal advocate for

---

[14] Maya Angelou, The Editors of Encyclopedia Britannica and updated by Adam Augustyn.
[15] Katherine Johnson Biography by Margot Lee Shetterly.

civil rights. She ran for President of the United States in 1972, becoming the first black major-party presidential candidate and the first woman to seek the democratic party's nomination for the presidency.[16]

Oprah Winfrey is a media mogul, philanthropist, and actress, screen director, is one of the most influential figures in American television history. Throughout her talk show, "The Oprah Winfrey Show," she became a powerful voice, addressing social issues and inspiring millions of viewers worldwide.

I remember a story in "Jet Magazine." Oprah encountered discrimination by a saleswoman about an expensive purchase abroad during her visit. Someone asked her if she could afford the item. That someone merely saw a woman of color, not knowing it was Oprah Winfrey.[17]

Her name is *Ms. Kay Henderson*, a petite woman I met on September 16, 2023, at the *Woman of Power Conference* in Riverdale, Georgia, at the Flint Community Center. I observed her passion and unconditional love in her

---

[16] Shirley Chisholm, Article Title: Shirley Chisholm Biography.Com Editors, Published April 2014.
[17] Oprah Winfrey Mair, George (2001). Oprah Winfrey: The Real Story. Citadel Press.

presentations before her guests and speakers at the event. I knew I had to wait for an opportune time to interview her for our upcoming book and about her community work.

She stopped at our Scribes at Work table and greeted Carol Dye and me. I asked her if I could interview her and she replied, "Yes." Excited, I watched her direct and redirect functions throughout the different stages of the preparation. I waited for the opportune time to interview her about the company.

The rain delayed the guests and speakers, so I could get the required information from her. After briefly sharing her trauma, she established a non-profit in 2013 to help women cope with their traumas.

The program is based on spiritual encounters with God and the interventional work of Ms. Kay's Vision Association Life Services in confronting their life trauma experiences. She celebrated their accomplishments during their trying times while receiving their bachelor's, master's, and doctorate degrees.

Ms. Kay has conducted her conferences six times in Columbus, Ohio, twice in Riverdale, Georgia, and will coordinate an upcoming conference in Pittsburgh, Pennsylvania, in 2024.

In the 19th century, it is hard to believe that the ugly head of discrimination still prevailed. Scientifically speaking, did the history changing impact of these courageous women fade? No. Their impact has not gone away. It will never go away. Hopefully, we will continue to be vigilant. With dignity, we can only hope our fight for freedom to live, work, and die for this country will enthusiastically endure.

It is amazing to see God walking with us when we are hurting, and how His continued pursuit of our love for Him and the concern for our fellowman never stops.

Today I thank God for the memories I have and share with my children, grandchildren, nieces, and nephews, when I visit them. I miss the bonding between older adults and younger people sharing their individual life journeys-back in the day, with everyone understanding their roots.

Let Me Tell You About "The Blue Room"

Excerpt from The Blue Room
By Dr. Geraldine Callahan & Tjuana Callahan

Many times, there are family secrets hiding among themselves or behind closed doors. In the rendering of this book, the Author exposes secrets. These hidden truths exist in plain sight, but we can't see them. It is the author's intention to pique your interest by giving you some personal family history.

I found out for myself that if you want answers to questions, you may be looking in all the wrong places. Some hidden things could be right in your face. You will have to look more closely. It may be hiding behind a wall; or it might just be there on the wall, waiting to be explored. Watch, Look and Listen. It might be in that very picture or on that same wall that holds the picture.

You might ask, what has The Blue Room got to do with anything? Well, I love the way you ask questions. Keep looking and you will find the answers. You've heard the old saying: "a picture is worth a thousand words." There's a wall dying to tell you about what you are wondering about; and this time "Curiosity Won't Kill the Cat." It will simply enlighten you. Mere curiosity as found in this book will inspire you to want more. You may find yourself standing "tip toe" in anticipation. The "Blue Room" will have you wondering about what comes next, and how do I get inside the room with the other readers.

What about hiding something in a dark, cold place such as a basement? But the basement was not the only place for hiding stuff. That too was where the main characters in this book routinely met to talk about secret things. The thought process was what's done in the dark won't come to the light. It's a secret. Who will know? But as I recap that phrase "I believe it goes like this: 'What's done in the dark will come to the light.'" Let's take a look and find out what's really going on..

My mother was the youngest girl of eleven children raised on a 200-acre farm in the south. As the older children married and moved away, they helped by sending for the younger children. By this means, all might have an opportunity to live a better lifestyle and get an education.

Therefore, at an early age, my mother was sent to live with her eldest sister's family in Macon, Georgia. This was a unique situation, as they were the overseers of the Blind Academy there in Macon. This afforded mom an opportunity to attend school and be raised in what was determined to be a better quality of life. She had what was considered to the very best of opportunities for a woman of color. That she lived with a sister and brother-in-law who were considered to be well off, established in the community, improved her ability to move forward.

The color of her skin was also a factor. That was vitally important in determining how far she could go. *You know, if you're white you're all right, if you're brown stick around, if you're black get back* (a cliché from back in the day).

Eventually, however, my mother would be sent onward to another sister's family in another progressive southern town to continue this upward trend. She was now able to move toward bettering her education and lifestyle. But this is where the story takes a turn.

That train of thought was cut off when "life" happened to her. No one ever expected that mom would get pregnant. Not once, but three times. I was the third conceived. Now I know that this was an act of God because the others did not survive.

Back in the day, the outhouse (Jon, or Out-Suite) was literally outdoors. "Slop jars," "tin tubs," "wash basins," "rub boards" and throwing the dishwater out the back door was the lifestyle. There was no plumbing available, but there was an element of pride because they owned these possessions.

If I sound sarcastic, it's because the truth has the power to set you free. It was called living off the land. Everyone had chores to do and learned from their experience. These criteria defined the formula for success.

If a young woman was with child, or as the Bible says: "with suck," she was a disgrace to the whole family. Therefore, she would simply be sent away to cover up the shame. The whole family participated in the secret cover up. As a result, she would be sent to live with a relative far away from prying eyes. The baby became the relative's child by simply blending in with the rest of the family.

This practice was common among family members to bring the younger ones into their families to nurture and help shape their futures. It was not considered being an imposition—it was just the way things were done.

Prayer for Change
By Tjuana Ladawn Callahan

Journal entry: March 18, 2000

Today, during the Women's Retreat in the State Park, the Lord spoke to me. The retreat was about spending time alone with God for refreshing, encouragement, and strength in the inner man. At 4:30 in the afternoon, I decided to take a walk all alone. As I started walking, the Lord directed me to the nature trails behind the Lodge. At first, I was afraid. I began to pray and dispatch guardian angels to go before me while canceling the assignments of demonic forces to cause any harm or distraction.

I continued to walk the trail for about 10 minutes. I discovered the tennis court in the middle of the woods. Nearby was a little wooden bridge going over a small stream with wooden handrails. I kneeled at the little bridge with arms folded over the handrails. Looking up into the tops of the trees, I said, "Praise the Lord trees! Do you love the Lord?" After a minute of that, I realized the trees don't have a soul. They don't love the Lord, nor are they able to. Yet, they are God's creation, obedient to His will.

Trees stand at attention before God, tall and strong. They do exactly what God intends providing a home for birds and animals, shelter for the ground. These majestic creations purify or provide oxygen for the air. So, I said, "Lord, I will praise You because You are worthy to be praised." I continued looking straight up into the treetops, then pass them into the sky. I began to confess:

> Lord, there are issues that have been plaguing me for a long, long time. Yet, I know my life can change and You can change it. In the past years, You accomplished in me what I thought was impossible.
>
> The first was deliverance from a lifestyle of fornication. The second was healing an acne skin problem. You have done these things and You can continue changing me. I am struggling with junkiness, uncleanness, being undisciplined, and laziness. I have taken the things you have given me for granted.
>
> I'm a poor steward of what I have. I now give You permission to take control and change my life. I'm asking for a radical, revolutionary change. I'm trusting You to do whatever it takes to help me that You may be able to use me. Change my life that I may operate in Your perfect will. I want to live up to the exciting potential that You have placed in me. I know You

have great acts to perform through me. I want to live in that realization.

I looked at my watch. Another 5 minutes passed. I realized I had been gone 25 minutes already. I got up to return when The Lord said, "Stay here with me a little longer. Walk with me just a little further. I want to tell you something." So, I crossed the little bridge and went further.

Lord, what do you want to show me? What do you want to tell me?

As I walked about twenty feet, I could hear a break in the stream and a gurgling sound. The Lord spoke to me again, "Stop here—listen—have a seat here." I sat at the edge of the stream. God said:

> I loved you all the while. You have been down for a long time. But I loved you for a long time. Now, I'm going to begin giving you the desires of your heart. Look for the best and live like a rich woman. I love you and I will give you the desires of your heart. Get up and go now.

I got up and began walking back. Then across the little bridge, I walked on. I shook the trees that were small enough for me to lean on at arm's length and gently swayed. It was my way of praising God through the trees. Looking up, I noticed the top branches waving back and forth as I leaned on the small tree trunks. The trail with a decline. Therefore, returning was an incline. God spoke again,

> I am bringing you up and out. You are not down anymore. As you leave this trail, I am bringing you up and out. When you come out of the trail, you will be a new person. You will be up and out. Your life is changing now. When you get to the top of the trail, you will not be the same.

Hallelujah! I'm changed. Thank You Lord!

Overcoming Challenges

By Donna J. Ware

It is a fact of life that each human being will have a challenge or many challenges to overcome during their lifetime. Sometimes our lives are "smooth as silk." Sometimes life is very hum-drum with no particular trial or test. At other times, we might have years of challenge after challenge. God tests our faith to what we perceive to be our limit. But shockingly, more challenges come. Test after test and tribulation after tribulation comes at us with no relief in sight. How can one withstand so much for so long?

The Bible promises us, "I have told you these things, so that in me you may have peace. In this world, you will have trouble. But take heart! I have overcome the world." (John 16:33, NIV) For any of us to think that we are exempt from this promise, is ludicrous. Instead of trying not to have life trials, we need to concentrate on what to do when they happen.

What does God consider being our best approach to overcome challenges? It is always great to see through God's perspective because He keeps score on our daily walk, and He has the final say.

God had me to pen a book entitled, *Growing UP In Gratefulness*. I completed my original manuscript and was ready to submit it for printing. At that moment, the Holy Spirit spoke to me and said, "That is not what gratefulness means to Me." I did not really understand then how critically important it was to teach "growth in gratefulness" solely from God's perspective. Because God demands that my teachings are 100% accurate from His viewpoint, He told me what to say about gratefulness.

You might think, what does gratefulness have to do with overcoming life's challenges? That answer if found in my second manuscript, the one I sent in for publication; the one the Holy Spirit dictated to me. The significance here is that the Holy Spirit taught me, "This thing called gratefulness seems to be the answer for many of life's pressing challenges."[18]

In a powerful book, *Knit Together*, the author wrote, "… we were created for gratitude. We are created to be grateful to our Creator for everything He's given us."[19] God showed

---

[18] Donna J. Ware. Growing UP In Gratefulness. "How to Grow UP In Gratefulness." (Delaware: KDP 2014) 69.
[19] Debbie Macomber. "Knit Together: Discover God's Pattern for Your Life." (New York: Faith Words, 2007) 173.

me how "gratefulness exceeds the verbal boundaries of thankfulness or thanksgiving."[20] Gratefulness is a stance we take in our hearts to trust God in everything that comes our way; knowing He is right there with us, He will grow us up in Him, believing that He alone "changes the times and seasons" in our lives. (See Daniel 2:21)

Author Sarah Ban Breathnach wrote,

> Gratitude unlocks the fullness of life. It turns what we have into enough and more. It turns denial into acceptance, chaos to order, confusion to clarity. It can turn a meal into a feast, a house into a home, a stranger into a friend. Gratitude makes sense of our past, brings peace for today, and creates a vision for tomorrow.[21]

Not only were we created to show gratefulness to God, but in our grateful attitudes, despite what life hands us, strength to "do all things through Christ Who strengthens [us]" will flow amid our circumstance. (See Philippians 4:13) No matter how grim, how destitute, how hopeless we are or feel, when we shower God with gratefulness *anyhow*, His hope, help, joy and peace will come our way. This hope, help,

---

[20] Donna J. Ware. Growing UP In Gratefulness. "Gratefulness." (Delaware: KDP, 2014) 21.

[21] Sarah Ban Breathnach, "Simple Abundance: A Daybook of Comfort and Joy." *Gratitude Journal* quoted Melodie Beattie. (New York: Warner Books, 1995) Jan. 14.

and joy do not always change our situation, but God promises "And the peace of God, which transcends all understanding, will guard your hearts and your minds in Christ Jesus." (See Philippians 4:7)

God's hope, help, joy, peace, and His strength as a reaction to your gratefulness is how you and I can withstand more challenges than we ever imagined we could endure. The Word says, "He gives strength to the weary, and increases the power of the weak." (Isaiah 40:29, NIV) Probably for most of us, being grateful no matter what, is *not* our most natural reaction. But God expects us to learn this secret power tool. He rewards us with His strength, His hope, His help, His joy, and His peace that surpasses all understanding. In my "Jesus Calling" devotional, Sarah Young wrote,

> Learn to live above your circumstances. This requires focused time with Me, *One who overcame the world.* Trouble and distress are woven into the very fabric of this perishing world. Only My Life in you can empower you to face this endless flow of problems with *good cheer.* [22]

---

[22] Sarah Young. Jesus Calling. March 13. "365 Day Devotional" (Nashville: Thomas Nelson, 2011) 76.

Life challenges are inevitable. How we choose to deal with them each day is a personal choice. In each instance, whether our challenge is physical, mental, emotional, or spiritual, you and I choose the outcome by choosing God's way or man's approach. In choosing to praise God, thank God, show gratefulness to God, we are claiming the Word, which says,

> Now to him who is able to do immeasurably more than all we ask or imagine, according to his power that is at work within us, to him be glory in the church and in Christ Jesus throughout all generations, for ever and ever! Amen. (Ephesians 3:20-21, NIV)

We cannot even blink our eyes by ourselves. Without God's power and perfect body operations plan in action, the simple blinking of our eyes cannot happen. We basically are powerless. We cannot make our circumstances or challenges change for the better. God is our help. Young wrote, "It is possible to enjoy Me and glorify Me in the midst of adverse circumstances. ... When things seem all wrong, trust Me anyway."[23]

---

[23] Young, 27.

In conclusion, the Scriptures say, "Rejoice always, pray continually, give thanks in all circumstances; for this is God's will for you in Christ Jesus." (1 Thessalonians 5:16-18, NIV) If you want to get better at facing life challenges, even long-term ones, learn to give God praise *anyhow*. Learn to take the stance of a grateful heart and keep standing in gratitude forever. Learn that God's perspective, His answers, and His perfect plans for your life are His very best for you. He will neither leave nor forsake you, but will be with you amid your gratefulness. To God be all the Glory.

Holy Living
By Donna J. Ware

The Word tells us, "Be ye holy, as I am holy." (See 1 Peter 1:16) Being preachers' kid and a preacher with preacher offspring, I know that a discourse on holy living, or righteousness, or holiness, is one that can bring any size congregation to dead silence. For over seven decades, I have witnessed that "hear a pin drop on the carpet" type of silence when whatever preacher or teacher boldly declared the necessity of holy living.

The *word* holy sounds out of reach to many of us. The actual *living* holy sounds even more difficult. But for Christians, this is non-negotiable. Our journeys-our daily lives must be about holy living, "Because it is written, Be ye holy; for I am holy." (1 Peter 1:16, KJV)

In my book, Growing UP in God, I composed a vocabulary list with definitions God taught me about spiritual maturity. Defined in that book, *holy* means "Without sin; pure; righteous; upright and clean in thought, word, and deed; God is the only One without sin, we all fall short, but are to daily strive for perfection."[24] One part of becoming spiritually mature is to consecrate our lives to each day being more and more like our holy God. For this to happen, the Holy Spirit must transform our minds from the world's thoughts to God's thoughts and ways. The Word says, "Do not conform to the pattern of this world, but be transformed by the renewing of your mind. Then you will be able to test and approve what God's will is—his good, pleasing and perfect will." (Romans 12:2, NIV)

In a GotQuestions.org article on holy living it states,

> This change of behavior begins on the inside with our attitude and mind-set. When our inner thought life, our purpose, and our character are changed into the image of Christ, our outward selves and outworking behavior will alter naturally. This process is the Holy Spirit's work of sanctification: "And we all, who with unveiled faces contemplate the Lord's glory, are being transformed into his image with ever-increasing glory, which comes from the Lord, who is the Spirit" (See 2 Corinthians 3:18).[25]

Sanctification, in the Bible, is another hard word for us

---

[24] Donna J. Ware, Growing UP in God, Vocabulary for holy. P 114, CreateSpace: SC, 2019.

[25] GotQuestions.org. How should we live in light of God saying, "Be holy for I am holy" (Leviticus 19:2; 1 Peter 1:16)? Accessed August 9, 2023.

to receive and achieve. It means "to make holy."[26] Sanctification is processed holiness. To be made holy is a lifetime series of being cleansed from all unrighteousness. We are washed by the Blood of the Lamb when each freedom from sin is made possible by discipline and pruning. "Human beings ultimately cannot sanctify themselves. The Triune God sanctifies. The Father sanctifies (See 1 Cor 1:30) by the Spirit (See 2 Thess 2:13; 1 Peter 1:2) and in the name of Christ (See 1 Cor 6:11)."[27]

In the theological sense, things are sanctified when they are used for the purpose God intends. "A human being is sanctified, therefore, when he or she lives according to God's design and purpose."[28] We Christians are to daily strive to live holy, sanctified, transformed lives. People should be able to see Jesus in us. Holiness has a "holy look" to the unbeliever. Sometimes our "holiness light" shines so brightly it is made visible by God to the human eye.

> Believers ought to be notably different from non-believers and their old selves because of their relationship with God through Jesus Christ. His holy

---

[26] BibleStudyTools.com. Sanctification. What is Sanctification? Bible Definition and Meaning (biblestudytools.com) Accessed August 10, 2023.
[27] Ibid. Bible Study Tools
[28] Ibid. Bible Study Tools

presence in our lives produces in us a loving obedience to God's Word, which ultimately forms God's character in us. If we are set apart for God's use, separated from our old, common way of living, we are following God's command to "be holy for I am holy."[29]

Some think holy rollers, sanctified holy, Pentecostal folks when thinking about holy, holiness, holy living people. But holy living and being holy are not limited to a particular denomination of Christians. Holy living is for all who know Christ as their Savior. All people are born of sin. We Christians have been forgiven and washed clean by God's saving grace. We are cleansed, made holy by our minds and hearts, being transformed and made right with God by calling on the precious Name of our Lord Jesus Christ. Hebrews reminds us to "Work at living in peace with everyone, and work at living a holy life, for those who are not holy will not see the Lord." (Hebrews 12:14, NIV)

Because the Holy Spirit abides inside of us Christians, we must daily strive to do all we can to avoid every evidence of sin, to "cleanse ourselves from everything that can defile

---

[29] Ibid. GotQuestions.org.

our body or spirit. And let us work toward complete holiness because we fear God." (See 2 Corinthians 7:1) Fearing God does not mean being afraid of Him, but it means reverencing Him; holding Him in our highest esteem. Realizing and acting like He is our Sovereign God and is worthy to be praised, worthy of our trying to walk a holy and righteous life.

In summing, God expects all of His believers to live as best we can, a holy, sanctified, justified, righteous life. We are to recognize the Holy Spirit's abiding within us and know that He cannot thrive in an unholy, defiled body, mind, or spirit. It is the Holy Spirit Who sanctifies us holy by the teaching, coaxing, convicting, disciplining, and pruning, all in the Name of Jesus Christ. "The Word says, "We have been rescued from our enemies so we can serve God without fear, in holiness and righteousness for as long as we live." (See Luke 1:74-75)

Reasons To Keep On Living
Donna J. Ware

Every day of my life, there are significant reasons to go on living. My "reasons" list is not always the same. Pain fills some days. Thankfully, some days joy and the joy of my salvation overflow my entire being (body, soul, and spirit). Whether pain-filled, joy-filled, sad, happy, glowing, dark, challenging, or success-filled days, that I am still alive to experience the moment is reason enough to keep on living.

When I wake with thankfulness in my heart, whisper a prayer of thanksgiving from my lips, and exude an overflow of gratefulness from my spirit, then even the most hoped for delights can cross my path. On February 15, 2013, I wrote the following prayer in my book Growing UP in Gratefulness, copied from one of my old gratefulness journals.

Dear God,

Thank You for a quiet day. I really, really could barely walk/limp today. Yesterday going to Publix, and my calf muscles were so sore, it was excruciating to walk & I have heel pain again as well. 'Oh Lord, how excellent is thy name in all the earth.' In all things, I count it joy, even the pain from the surgery. I am alive to feel it; for this, I praise You. Thanks for all my blessings & those for each of my family members & friends. You are awesome, God! Humbly, Donna J. [30]

A much-loved song, delicious book, delectable recipe, phone call from a loved one, picture sent via text or email, "food for thought" moment, beautiful sunshiny day, rare steady barometric day with only occasional pain, finding an item I need on a great sale, learning an answer to a medical mystery that doctors could not uncover, or a multitude of other grace-filled things might complete my day. These and unexpected, God-ordained happenings give me more reasons to keep on living. For all things in my every day, gratefulness flows from the depths of my soul.

You might wonder why I would take the time to write about my reasons to keep on living. "Is she depressed?" you might ask. No, I am not *depressed*, but I am *impressed* by how lovingly, carefully, attentively, and kindly God takes care of me. No matter what our circumstances; from the most desperate dire straits to our unbelievable prosperity of body,

---

[30] Donna J. Ware. Growing UP In Gratefulness, "How To Grow UP In Gratefulness." Thus Far Series, Vol 2. P. 68. DE: Middletown, 2014.

soul, and spirit, God, the Maker and Creator of all humanity, loves you, cares about you, and waits on you to send pleas for help and praises of adoration. The Word tells us,

> How precious to me are your thoughts, God!
>   How vast is the sum of them!
> I was counting them,
>   They would outnumber the grains of sand—
>   When I awake, I am still with you. (Psalm 139:17-18, NIV)

What the psalmist wrote is, how unique, how incredible your thoughts are about me, LORD. That you take one moment of Your time to focus on me and the concerns of my heart is mind-boggling. The Psalmist penned,

> Where can I go from your Spirit?
>   Where can I flee from your presence?
> If I go up to the heavens, you are there;
>   If I make my bed in the depths, you are there.
> If I rise on the wings of the dawn,
>   If I settle on the far side of the sea,
> Even there, your hand will guide me,
>   Your right hand will hold me fast. (Psalm 139: 7-10, NIV)

I have learned through trial and error when my life situation is one where praise and gratefulness seem preposterous, incomprehensible, and the most difficult to do, that is when I should muster all the inner strength I can and praise God anyhow. When my "praises go up, His blessings will come down" to me. If all I can whisper is "Jesus, Jesus, Jesus," the Holy Spirit knows my unverbalized concerns, interprets them, and takes them to heaven. Jesus Christ intercedes for me by petitioning God the Father on my behalf.

God's reason for reacting to you, me, and everyone has not changed. We are born into this world to serve God's purpose for us. If you have accepted Jesus as your Lord and Savior, then knowing your purpose becomes crystal clear. You realize as I have, my life is not about me but about what God wants to do through me for His glory. He said, "But I have raised you for this very purpose, that I might show you **my** power and that **my** name might be proclaimed in all the earth." (Exodus 9:16, NIV)

So, the most important reason for us to keep living is not about us but about God, His purposes, and His glory. No matter if incarcerated, living your days in an iron lung, if family, friends, or strangers persecute you; if you are lying in a hospital bed, cannot talk, or can speak freely, cannot move or move very well, if you live in an abusive situation, or a loving home, if you are very young or anciently old or any age in between, God desires for you to spread the Good News that Jesus Saves. He waits for you to ask Him what you can do for Him. He expects you to learn to find a glimmer of hope in Him, to focus on His face versus your challenge, to praise Him and wait on Him, worship Him, and grow in Him, all for His glory, no matter what.

The Job of the Book of Job in the Bible suffered the unimaginable for seemingly no reason. Yet, Job never turned his back on God. Most of us could quickly think he had no reason to keep on living. But against all odds, he held on to God's unchanging hands. He did not feel blessed. By no stretch of the imagination, did he seem to be blessed. But he was. And for His loyalty to God, for not cursing God and dying - as his wife suggested, God blessed Job immensely beyond where it all began.

> The LORD blessed the latter part of Job's life more than the former. …
> After this, Job lived a hundred and forty years; he saw his children and their children to the fourth generation.
> And so Job died, an older man and full of years. (Job 42:12, 16-17, NIV)

Learn To Pray With Power
By Donna J. Ware

Before your end, hopefully you realize that the most powerful prayer is the prayer we call "The Lord's Prayer"—the prayer Jesus gave to His Apostles in response to their query as to how they should pray. It is a short, concise, perfect prayer because in it you ask God's will to be done in your life. In essence, you give over your ways and thoughts to His, resulting in a major stride in your spiritual growth.

Jesus said to pray this way: Matthew 6:9-13,

9 After this manner therefore pray ye: Our Father which art in heaven, Hallowed be thy name.

10 Thy kingdom come. Thy will be done in earth, as it is in heaven.

11 Give us this day our daily bread.

12 And forgive us our debts, as we forgive our debtors.

13 And lead us not into temptation, but deliver us from evil: For thine is the kingdom, and the power, and the glory, forever. Amen. (KJV)

If you pray no more than, "Thy will be done," you have prayed a power-filled, deeply humbled, highly reverent, and spiritually mature prayer. God knows your needs before you speak them. Matthew 6:8 says, *"… for your father knoweth what things ye have need of, before ye ask him."* (KJV) The Prayer of Jabez found in 1 Chronicles 3:10 says, "… enlarge my territory." (KJV)

When you make prayer a disciplined part of your life, God will enrich your spiritual life. This discipline is discussed concisely in Richard Foster's book, *Celebration of the Disciplines.*[31] The title is a wonderful clue for what awaits those who will dedicate themselves to the spiritual disciplines—the requisite tools for spiritual growth.

You can enjoy a highly blessed celebration with the Lord; you can attain closeness with God like none you could ever have imagined. Because of your closer walk with God, most times both the "small stuff" and the larger challenges will not disturb your rest in Him.

This is not to say that the devil will not try to distract you. Nevertheless, you will know that "…greater is he that is in [you] than he that is in the world." (1 John 4:4b, KJV) And, you will know the One who is your Rock, Sword, and your Shield. The Word says,

____

[31] Richard Foster. Celebration of Disciplines.

The Lord is my rock, and my fortress, and my deliverer; my God, my strength, in whom I will trust; my buckler, and the horn of my salvation, and my high tower. (Psalm 18:2, KJV)

When I examine this verse, this is what I hear in my spirit:

- God is my **rock** - my large, dependable, stable Heavenly Father.

- God is my **fortress** - my impenetrable, fortified protection.

- God is my **deliverer** - the One who puts a halt to the devil's attacks, removes stumbling blocks, and lifts me up and away from danger.

- God is my **strength** - my Source of support and power.

- God is my **trusted One** - the One I can always rely on to care for me with the very best care possible; to open doors no man can shut; to be a lamp unto my feet and light unto my path.

- God is my **buckler -** my shield for the enemy's arrows.

- God is my **horn of salvation** - the mighty Redeemer by whose power-filled blood I am saved.

- God is my **high tower** - my high place where I can hide where danger cannot reach me.

I do not know about you, but for me, this solitary verse offers so much peace that I know for certain I can rest while God fights my battles, paves the way, and opens the doors for my destiny and spiritual growth. I take great comfort in praying to a God who is so awesome.

Please note that your prayers do not have to be filled with intellectual prowess. To be powerful, your prayers must solely be straight from the heart. Prayer is merely a conversation with you and God. Pray your heart and you have prayed with power.

When you pray, "Thy will be done", you are offering praise to God that He is the only One in whom you trust; you are acknowledging His power, His wisdom, and His sovereignty. You are recognizing that in this world, we are fighting spiritual battles and whatever God desires will rule. In order to do your part in these spiritual battles, the Word says for you to:

[10] Finally, my brethren, be strong in the Lord, and in the power of his might.

¹¹ Put on the whole armour of God, that ye may be able to stand against the wiles of the devil.

¹² For we wrestle not against flesh and blood, but against principalities, against powers, against the rulers of darkness of this world, against spiritual wickedness in high places.

¹³ Wherefore take unto you the whole armour of God, that ye may be able to withstand in the evil day, having done all, to stand.

¹⁴ Stand therefore, having your loins girt about with truth, and having on the breastplate of righteousness;

¹⁵ And your feet shod with the preparation of the gospel of peace;

¹⁶ Above all, taking the shield of faith, wherewith ye shall be able to quench all the fiery darts of the wicked.

¹⁷ And take the helmet of salvation, and the sword of the Spirit, which is the word of God:

¹⁸ Praying always with all prayer and supplication in the Spirit, and watching thereunto with all perseverance and supplication for all saints; (KJV)

To God be all the glory.[32]

---

[32] Donna J. Ware. Growing UP in God. Chapter *Four Adulthood in Christ*. P. 57-60, CreateSpace: SC, 2019.

Where Are The Greatest Minds?

By Patricia Ann Callahan Morris

Where can you find the individuals who had extraordinary minds? Reflecting on this, far too many extraordinary minds are unfortunately in cemeteries. The first person who comes to mind is Nelson Mandela. Imprisoned for so long, many thought him dead.

Nelson Mandela, a humble man living in South Africa, became an anti-apartheid leader and politician who served for five years as the first president of South Africa. What was interesting about Mandela. "A good leader can engage in a debate frankly and thoroughly, knowing that at the end he and the other side must be closer, and thus emerge stronger. You don't have that idea when you are arrogant, superficial, and uninformed."[33]

It would have been interesting to sit down and listen to his stories about the importance of freedom for he and his people in their own country, and how he and endured and overcame horrific obstacles while imprisoned for an

---

[33] Nelson Mandela– An interview with Oprah for O Magazine, April 2001.1.

incredible twenty-seven years, losing the freedom for which he fought. Mandela received over 250 awards, including the Nobel Peace Prize, and spent the years after his service as president, in the fight against poverty and the HIV/AIDS battle in his country.

Albert Einstein a German-born theoretical physicist, was widely known to be one of the greatest and most influential scientists of all time. Best known for developing the *theory of reality*. What intrigued me about him was the beliefs about never sharing with anyone other than your doctor, therapist, or other trained professional of your problems. Let us look at two out of five things Albert Einstein said about your problems or ideals with someone you do not share with them and understand his logic and think about his advice. "Everyone has a problem, but if yours becomes so alarming, others will leave theirs and debate yours. There are things you can share with people and some things you never share with people no matter how close they are to you."[34]

I am sure we all have someone with whom we have shared, and later heard someone speak about what you

---

[34] Albert Einstein, www.#einsteinquotes #alberteinsteinquotes #lifequotes #wisequotes 5 Things Never Share with Anyone 2, Accessed October 2, 2023.

shared with your friend or acquaintance. My mother would say, "You know your words when you hear them." Sadly, people like to have something to gossip about. It is the truth. It happens all the time - in general conversations at the workplace, family, and friend gatherings. It can even be one in your family who you can count on them sharing about your business and not their own. So, if you can keep something private everything else will fall into place.

Since I have had a great interest in poetry, upon becoming a member of a writers' guild, I highlighted James Mercer Langston Hughes.

James Langton Hughes was an American poet, social activist, novelist, playwright, and columnist from Joplin, Missouri. I would like to share about this one poem I related to for being a dreamer. The poem is entitled "Dreams." It is a two-stanza poem which highlights the value of dreams. It presents two situations that revolve around the loss of those dreams.

Dreams

Hold fast to dreams
For if dreams die
Life is a broken-winged bird
That cannot fly.

Hold fast to dreams
For when dreams go
Life is a barren field
Frozen with snow.[35]

---

[35] Langston Hughes, "Dreams" from *The Collected Works of Langston Hughes*. Copyright © 2002 by Langston Hughes. Reprinted by permission of Harold Ober Associates, Inc.

Is It God's Favor Or Not?

By Donna J. Ware

In September 2023, I published a book, Growing UP in God's Favor. The following is a direct quote from a portion of this work.

"God changes caterpillars into butterflies, sand into pearls and coal into diamonds using time and pressure. He's working on you too."[36] Sometimes favor does not seem like, feel like, look like favor. I have been living this statement for the past three years.

Over ten years ago, God showed me, and the Holy Spirit taught me about God's favor. At that time, I accepted favor as mine, and have lived expecting favor-in-action ever since then. Recently, I realized after much prayer and meditation that even with the relentless challenge of pain, God's favor is in action each day for me. I may not feel like it, but God never leaves my side. True to His Word, He knows His plans for my life. (See Jeremiah 29:11) A prosperous, healthy, unharmed life with a future is one of those promises.

---

[36] Rick Warren, https://quotlr.com/quotes-about-god%27s-favor. Accessed 07.29.2023.

Without going into great detail right now, this faith walk part of my life's journey began three years ago with my first foot surgery. Because of a miscommunication involving lack of sufficient milligrams of post-surgery pain medication, that first night at home I thought with each breath I would die, my heart would stop beating from the intensity of the pain.

This may not sound like favor when you read this, but it was. My prayer partner, Donna J. Marshall (gone to Glory 2022) gave me a devotional in 2016. For God's reasons, on July 14, 2023, that devotional struck a chord so loud, so hard, with such resonance that I had to type it out to store on my screen saver. I open it and read it whenever I need the reassurance of His favor in action during this challenging season of my life.

I feel led to share Sarah Young's powerful words here with you at this teachable moment. If you are amid a challenge of any sort, may these words comfort and guide you as well.

From Jesus Calling (devotional by Sarah Young - July 14)

Reading this devotion this year (2023) I could hear the voice of God whispering to me.

Donna,

KEEP WALKING with ME along the path I have chosen for you. Your desire to live close to Me is a delight to My heart. I could instantly grant you the spiritual riches you desire, but that is not My way for you. Together we will forge a pathway up the high mountain. The journey is arduous at times, and you are weak. Someday you will dance light-footed on the high peaks; but for now, your walk is often plodding and heavy. All I require of you is to take the next step, clinging to My hand for strength and direction. Though the path is difficult and the scenery dull at the moment, there are sparkling surprises just around the bend. Stay on the path I have selected for you. It is truly the *path of Life*.[37]

Priscilla Shirer said, "What might God be trying to grow in your character or cement in your relationship with Him by keeping you separated from some things you want but don't yet have?[38] When we think God is not working on our behalf, when we feel He is ignoring our prayers, or He is taking too long to answer, we need to stop and reflect on

---

[37] Sarah Young. "Jesus Calling: Enjoying Peace in His Presence." Nashville: Thomas Nelson, 2011, 205.
[38] Priscilla Shirer. https://www.azquotes.com/author/46257-Priscilla_Shirer, Accessed July 21, 2023.

what is actually happening. We need to recognize His favor *is* quietly in action for us.

Let me make God's favor intentions for us crystal clear. His favor is experienced by Christians when ways are made out of no way, when we get that job when all signs indicated we would not, when money to pay our bills appears out of thin air, when the doctors say go home to put our affairs in order because we have months or weeks to live, and we are still here decades later, when that wandering son or daughter suddenly returns home after years of our pleas to heaven, when all the right doors open and the wrong ones close, when we could have been killed in that accident but God spared us for our destiny walk with Him. All the "non-coincidences" in our lives, the mysterious provisions, protections, and pronouncements that happen for our good despite the odds, these things are all God's favor.

"MAMA SAID"

SAGE ELDERS' ROUNDTABLE QUOTES

MAMA SAID

The following pages are memorable quotes from our mamas, grandmamas, aunties, sisters, and cousins — but mainly our mamas. Since our guild is composed of senior ladies, our wise and sometimes strong or startling quotes have been garnered throughout our lifetimes.

FAMILY & FRIENDSHIP

- "Mama said know your friends from your acquaintances because everyone who smiles in your face is not your friend." – **Collins**

- **Morris's** *mama said about friendship:*

- "A friend gives you advice that is in your best interests."

- "A friend is someone you can confide in about your pain and feel it, not and tell others behind your back."

- "A genuine friend has your back through good and down times."

- "A friend accepts who you are."

- "A real friend will tell you the truth. Even if you don't like it."

- "A loyal friend will come and see you when you are sick."

- "A good friend encourages you to achieve your dreams and goals."

- "A genuine friend will accept you and even find your quirks and imperfections as a person of worth and beauty."

- "A loyal friend, you feel comfortable with in their presence."

- "A loyal friend is one you may not have spoken to for a while. They are glad to hear from you."

- "It is us against the world. We must stick together." (spoken to her three sons after divorce) – **Ware**

- "God handpicked *you* to be in this family." – **Ware**

- "God, family, and friends is the best life can offer us." – **Ware**

- "A family that prays together, stays together." - **Ware**

<u>BLESSINGS, TRUST, and PRAYER</u>

- "The Lord always makes a way somehow."– **Lee**

- "Sometimes, God has to drag us to our blessings." – **Ware**

- "Trust GOD in everything you do." – **Collins**

- "Praise the Lord, everybody! Oh, you can do better than that! I said, PRAISE THE LORD EVERYBODY." – **Callahan**

- "Prayer changes things." – **Ware**

- "Presence is ministry." – **Callahan**

- "Do not holler at your child. One day he will be a blessing." – **Callahan**

- "My kids cut their spiritual teeth on prayers and fasting." – **Ware**

- "I'm so blessed, my blessed is blessed!" - **Ware**

<u>DOING RIGHT</u>

- "Always do the right thing and God will do the rest." – **Ware**

- "A hard head will make a soft behind." – **Lee**

- "When are you going to stop making the same mistakes?" – **Callahan**

- "Am I right about it?" – **Tooks**

- "A liar will steal, and a thief will lie." – **Lee**

- "I hope me die." (Translated: *I would rather die than tell a lie. This is what my Granny Goins always said.*) – **Ware**

- "What you say… and you better not say it again!" – **Tooks**

- "Keep your powders dry." (*Translated: Do nothing you cannot tell me about. What Grandma Lee said.*) – **Ware**

- "You are not the boss of me!" – **Tooks**

- "Do the very best that you can, and you will be okay." – **Callahan**

- "There is nothing better than being in God's perfect will versus His permissive will." – **Ware**

EVERYDAY LIVING

- "An beatin' na'an." (Translated: *One is better than nothing at all.*) – **Callahan**

- "Boy! comb your nappy head before them naps beat your brains out."(My older cousin said this.) - **Dye**

- "Nothing beats a failure but a try." – **Collins**

- "Hard work never kills you." – **Lee**

- "That's neither here nor there."- **Tooks**

- "No pain, no gain." – **Ware**

- "Seasonal allergies, such as hay fever, can worsen certain health conditions in older adults and make them feel less comfortable during specific seasons." - **Morris**

- "Save ten cents out of every dollar." – **Collins**

- "You better watch your mouth." – **Lee**

- "Don't call my name anymore! Reply, "OK Mom." – **Tooks**

- "Seasons themselves do not directly cause aging. They can influence various factors that impact the aging process, including the sun exposure, temperature, lifestyle, and health conditions." - **Morris**

- "Don't let me go upside your head and bust you in your back!" – **Tooks**

- "You can kill with kindness." – **Ware**

- "Don't fight with boys because they can hit harder."- **Lee**

- "Don't let the left hand know what is in the right hand." – **Collins**

- "The answer is NO, and I dare you to ask me again!" – **Tooks**

- "The hurrier I go, the behinder I get." – **Ware**

- "Everything that glitters ain't gold." – **Collins**

- "I don't care if you get 6' tall, I'll take you down and put my foot on your neck!" – **Tooks**

- "It's important for older adults to be mindful of seasonal effects and take care to maintain their health and well-being throughout the year." - **Morris**

- "You don't tell your mama everything." – **Lee**

- "What?! I'm the momma!" – **Tooks**

- "Staying physically active and socially engaged is crucial for healthy aging." - **Morris**

- Talking to him is just like talking to a brick wall." (Grandma said this). - **Dye**

- "I brought you here, and I'll take you out!" – **Tooks**

- "The availability of seasonal fruits and vegetables can impact an individual's diet." - **Morris**

- "You are just a bald-faced lie!" – **Tooks**

- "Hold that thought." - **Ware**

<u>DESTINY</u>

- "When you get married, always have your own bank account." – **Collins**

- "You just trifling." – **Tooks**

- "You know the fruit doesn't fall far from the tree." – **Callahan**

- "Seasonal variations in sunlight exposure can have a significant impact on aging." – **Morris**

- "You can do anything or be anything you want to be. You might have to try harder, or cry more tears, but you can do anything you want." (My Dad told me this from my birth until his death, 2003) - **Ware**

- "Put on some decent clothes before you go out and look like you somebody!" (Grandma said this.) – **Dye**

- "The effects of UV radiation and the different temperatures can affect how our bodies function." - **Morris**

- "There's nothing new under the sun."- **Ware**

- Seasonal Affect Disorder (SAD): "Some people, particularly older individuals, may experience

Seasonal Affective Disorder, a type of depression that occurs at specific times of the year, typically during the fall and winter months when daylight hours are shorter." - **Morris**

- "I'm excited about your future!" – **Callahan**

- "Work like you're working for God." – **Ware**

- "There are only two ways to live your life. One is as though nothing is a miracle. The other is as though everything is a miracle."(Quoting Albert Einstein) – **Ware**

- "Good help is HARD to find!"- **Ware**

<u>LOVE</u>

- "I'm so proud of my girls!" – **Callahan**

- "The way to a man's heart is his stomach." – **Lee**

- "We ask of you your love and respect for us." – **Callahan**

- "Love conquers all." - **Ware**

- "Y'all want some swimps?" – **Tooks**

- "Come here and give me some sugar." – **Callahan**

- Mama said, "Life is the best gift your dad and I have given you ALL." – **Callahan**

- "Nothing is as good as being loved by Jesus." - **Ware**

- "Be kind, especially to those who aren't kind to you."- **Ware**

- "I love you. Good night." – **Callahan**

- "Jesus loves you!"-**Ware**

CONCLUSION

We are a group of writers dedicated to your being blessed by our God-given works. Our guild is based on the Word found in 1 Corinthians 2:13, "This is what we speak, not in words taught us by human wisdom but in words taught by the Spirit, explaining spiritual realities with Spirit-taught words." (NIV)

Our works are to teach, guide, inspire, and to inform you dear readers, all in obedience to God and for His glory. Our founder, Donna Ware, shares with you a Rhema word God spoke to her about thirty years ago. These words are applicable for what we as a writers' guild do today. That word is, "You cannot teach what you do not know, and you have not lived."[39]

Just for you: DEFINITION OF RHEMA -

rhéma (ῥῆμα in Greek); that which is spoken, what is uttered in speech or writing; **1** an utterance (individually, collectively, or specifically); **2** the word by which something

---

[39] Rhema words God spoke to SAW Founder and Author, Donna J. Ware in the 1990's.

is commanded, directed, or enjoined; **3** something that is spoken clearly and vividly, in unmistakable terms and in an undeniable language. In the New Testament, the word *rhema* carries the idea of a quickened word [word spoken into the spirit of a person by the Holy Spirit].[40]

In this work, we shared portions of our life journeys to inspire you in your daily walk. We became "open books" in order to help you in any way our stories could. In the words of Maya Angelou, from her book, *I Know Why the Caged Bird Sings*, "There is no greater agony than bearing an untold story inside you." Each of us who contributed to this compiled work has similar and dissimilar stories to tell. Our journeys though maybe worlds apart in appearance, are similar in that we each lived life – we each walked and continue to walk pre-destined life pathways.

We have shared experiences that have taught us what Roy T. Bennett speaks of in *The Light in the Heart*. Hopefully, you too can "Start each day with a positive thought and a grateful heart."[41] We each have learned to varying degrees what Nicholas Sparks wrote in *The Last Song*,

> I have faith that God will show you the answer. But you have to understand that sometimes it takes a

---

[40] Rick Renner, Sparkling Gems From the Greek (Tulsa: Teach All Nations, 2003), 78.

[41] Roy Bennett. www.goodreads.com/quotes/grateful. Accessed October23, 2023.

while to be able to recognize what God wants you to do. That's how it often is. God's voice is usually nothing more than a whisper, and you have to listen very carefully to hear it. But other times, in those rarest of moments, the answer is obvious and rings as loud as a church bell.[42]

As you walk through your life journey, dear reader, may you never forget these words of Bill Keane: "Yesterday is history, tomorrow is a mystery, today is a gift of God, which is why we call it the present."[43] Please make the best use as you possibly can of your daily gift of life.

Helen Keller was a person who could have been swal-lowed up by her disabilities, but she instead had the inward sight to make this statement, "When one door of happiness closes, another opens; but often we look so long at the closed door that we do not see the one which has been opened for us."[44] We Sage Elders hope you will not waste the moments of your precious life looking back, dwelling on regrets, or missing God's favored opportunities for you.

Corrie ten Boom shared with us to, "Never be afraid to

---

[42] Nicholas Sparks. The Last Song. www.goodreads.com/quotes/work. Accessed October 15,2023.

[43] Bill Keane. www.goodreads.com/quotes/life. Accessed October15, 2023.

[44] Helen Keller. www.goodreads.com/quotes/life. Accessed October15, 2023.

trust an unknown future to a known God."[45] We pray God's grace and His blessings in your life for right now, tomorrow, and forevermore.

---

[45] Corrie ten Boom. www.goodreads.com/quotes/life. Accessed October 15, 2023.

CONTRIBUTING AUTHORS

Dr. Geraldine Callahan

The late Dr. Geraldine Callahan is the author of *Write the Vision – Volume One* and *Remembering Doc* (about Dr. Frederick G. Sampson, II, her mentor). She also compiled, edited, and typeset *The Seedline, An Old Testament Survey* by Dr. Grant R. Carter.

She was a founding member, and previously served as group leader and as secretary of our writers guild, S.A.W. In her honor, Tjuana-her daughter, completed her mother's last unfinished work, *The Blue Room*. Also, she was the recipient of numerous awards in recognition of her dedication to the church and community-at-large. As a loyal servant of Jesus Christ, her motto was: "REACH, TEACH, PREACH & KEEP."

Tjuana Ladawn Callahan

The lessons gained along life's journey must be shared. Tjuana "Ladawn" Callahan is the author of two collections of poetry – *Ain't God Good!* (1997) and *Moving Out of Dream Castles* (2006). After years of silence, this author realized that the road from fear to faith must not be traveled alone. *The Love Life of Fear and Paranoia* was released in 2017. Ladawn is a follower of Christ, transforming from a lifestyle of fears and depression to a mindset of love and faith. She is a former group leader of the S.A.W. writers guild, and currently serves as treasurer. She is also a contributor to the guild's first group compiled book and for this second one.

Lillian S. Collins

Lillian Collins is the author of "To Hell and Back, Hell is Real" and registered into the United States Library of Congress but is currently unpublished. She is a former group leader and has served as secretary.

She won an award for her short story "In the Night" that is currently published in this book. Most of her writings are creative short stories to mentor young people about life. All of her work is fiction. This is her first time being published.

Carol D. Dye

As a retired Professional Assistant for Education, The Lord put me on a path to compose my first book; *Journey Through Psalms 111-150 Decoding God's Word* in 2012. Since then, I have two other books *Proverbs: In Search Of Unscrambling Wisdom, and Psalm 119: Word Decoding.*

As a result of the previous books, God laid on my heart to explore puzzle books and journals. I have just released a comprehensive multiple year usage *"Christmas Planner."* I'm praying that these books will be a blessing to those who are seeking to invest time with the Lord and as a benefit challenging the memory of his word. She is also a game and puzzle writing contributor for the guild's first book and for this one.

Trudie V. Lee

Trudie V Lee is a writer, teacher, social worker and spoken word artist. Along with her husband, she has written and produced a documentary, an educational film and several inspirational videos that inform, entertain and motivate people of different ethnicities, ages and genders.

Some of her most recent works include a children's book, *How BIG Is Your TRUCK GreShawn?* and an inspirational series for older people. Although she has a passion to write and produce, it does not interfere with or replace the joy she experiences with her grandchildren, family, and church.

Patricia Ann Callahan Morris

Patricia Morris is a retired Registered Occupational Therapist. For thirty-seven years she served as Director of Rehabilitation Departments, was an Adjunct Professor, Author, and Co-Author of works related to Physical Medicine, and reared her two sons. She joined the Scribes at Work writers' guild authors to address humankind's life journeys.

Patricia addresses faith, trust, purpose, wisdom, obedience, and understanding found in our first work *Inkwell's Dips and Drips of Life's Wisdom.* She has also published, *"Wut Do I Know,"* for children struggling with The Common Core Standards in the areas of Mathematics and Language. She is a former and present group leader of the writers' guild, S.A.W. She is also a contributor for the guild's first group compiled book and for this second one. Pat's website: www.wutdoiknow.com Her Facebook and Twitter can be accessed at patmorris60@yahoo.com.

Annette Tooks

Annette Tooks is an ordained minister, a called prophetess and licensed chaplain of the Gospel of Jesus Christ. The mom of three children, she is also the author of *Psalms of the*

Soul and co-author of *Shattered*. She hosted an Atlanta Christian radio show "Women of Standard," was the co-host "Real Men Talk" and "Soul Out Ministry" from 2005 to 2010. Annette is a retired realtor of over twenty-five years. The author loves and teaches the Gospel of Jesus Christ She is also a writing contributor for the guild's first book and for this one.

Denise Vicks

I learned a lot about myself during this life I was given. "There but for the grace of God go I," is one of my favorite quotes. I have caught myself using it often during my walk of life. God constantly shows me how much He has given me and how blessed I am. Despite my Fibromyalgia, and multiple other conditions, God has blanketed me with His loving grace. Denise writes Christian fiction mystery. She served as the 2021-2022 S.A.W. writing guild leader, and is also a writing contributor for the guild's first book and wrote poetry for this one. She was the daughter of our dearly departed beloved Adele Vicks who contributed to our first group book.

Donna J. Ware

The 2013 founding leader, 2017 and 2023 secretary for the inspirational writers' guild S.A.W., God-called ordained and licensed preacher, teacher, missionary, prophetess, church planter and master-degreed Christian counselor, Donna remains in awe of God's works brought forth from the depths of the guild members' souls. She is the author and self-publisher of *God Talk 101 and Sweet Jesus*–facilitated her to be inducted as a 2020 Texas Indie Author.

Donna has published eight other books. She is the editor and typesetter for four volumes of poetry and several other authors' books. She published a magazette "Faith, Hope, and Charity," and for her pastor mom she compiled, typeset, and published a newsletter entitled "Heaven Readiness."

Donna final edited and typeset our S.A.W. guild's first and second group compiled books. She is a contributing writer for both works.

In 2023 she published *Parts Room Revised Edition* and *Growing UP in God's Favor*. Her prayer is to fulfill - for God's glory, her pre-ordained writer's destiny. Email Donna at: 1grace house555@gmail.com OR you may link to her books and author page at: amazon.com/author/donnajware.

Other Books by the Authors

<u>Dr. Geraldine Callahan</u> -

- *Remembering "Doc": A tribute to Dr. Frederick George Sampson, II*

- *"The Seedline": Old Testament Survey (By Dr. Grant Carter with Dr. Geraldine Callahan)*

<u>Tjuana Ladawn Callahan</u> -

- *The Love Life of Fear and Paranoia: From Heartbreak to Healing*

- *Moving Out of Dream Castles...Where Dreams Become Reality*

- *Ain't God Good?*

<u>Carol Dye</u> -

- *Proverbs: In Search of Unscrambling Wisdom*

- *Psalm 119: Word Decoding*

- *Christmas Planner*

<u>Trudie Lee</u> -

- *How BIG is Your TRUCK GreShawn*

Patricia Ann Callahan Morris -

- *"Wut Do I Know?"*

Annette Tooks -

- *Psalms of the Soul*

- *Shattered (co-author)*

Donna J. Ware -

- *God Talk 101*

- *Sweet Jesus*

- *EGI Church Constitution and Bylaws*

- *Growing UP in God (Overview)*

- *Growing UP in God (Workbook)*

- *Growing UP in Gratefulness*

- *Rapture Readiness*

- *Parts Room*

- *Parts Room Revised Edition*

- *Growing UP in God's Favor*

Sage Elders *(Pen name for S.A.W. guild writers)* -

- *Inkwells: Dips and Drips of Life's Wisdom*

Individual Books Members Of Scribes at Work (S.A.W.) To be Released In 2024:

- *The Blue Room: If Walls Could Talk* – Tjuana Ladawn Callahan

- *A Prayer Journal* – Carol D. Dye
- *Scramble Word Book* – Carol D. Dye

- *Suit Yourself EVALENA (I HATE Homework)* - Trudie V. Lee

- *Wut Do I Know?* (Grades 2-8) – Patricia Ann Callahan Morris
- *2024 Mothers Are Resilient Calendar* – Patricia Ann Callahan Morris
- *Mama Said* – Patricia Ann Callahan Morris

- *The Dozen* – Donna J. Ware
- *Knowledge Is Power* – Donna J. Ware

www.ingramcontent.com/pod-product-compliance
Lightning Source LLC
Chambersburg PA
CBHW071413150726
48000CB00001B/299